Practical Chinese Reader
Elementary Course: Book I

Traditional Character Edition

D0002223

Cheng & Tsui Company

實 用 漢 語 課 本

Practical Chinese Reader
Elementary Course: Book I

繁 體 字 本

Traditional Character Edition

第 一 冊

Beijing Language Institute

Cheng & Tsui Company

2004 Printing

Published by

Cheng & Tsui Company
25 West Street
Boston, MA 02111-1213 USA
Fax (617) 426-3669
www.cheng-tsui.com
"Bringing Asia to the World"™

Traditional Character Edition ISBN 0-88727-229-0

Supplementary materials for *Practical Chinese Reader,* including exercise
book, writing workbook, computer software, videotapes, and audio materials,
are available from the publisher.

Printed in the United States of America

Publisher's Note to 1995 Edition

With the help of our many wonderful customers, we are happy to be able to supply you with a much more thoroughly proofread and edited version of the Traditional Character Edition of *Practical Chinese Reader Book 1* and *Book 2*. In addition to correcting typographical and *pinyin* tone mark errors, we have included at the bottom of each page, in parentheses, the corresponding pages in the Simplified Character Edition. With this ready cross-reference, we hope that it will be easier to use the audio cassette tapes which refer only to page numbers in the Simplified Character Edition.

We would also like to inform our readers that vocabulary indexes to these two texts are provided at the end of the respective supplement, *Practical Chinese Reader I: Patterns and Exercises* and *Practical Chinese Reader II: Patterns and Exercises.*

Although we received help from teachers everywhere, we owe a special debt of gratitude for the extra efforts made by Professor James Dew of Johns Hopkins University, Professor John Rohsenow of the University of Illinois-Chicago, Professor Scott McGinnis of the University of Maryland-College Park, and Professor Zu-yan Chen of the State University of New York-Binghamton in assuring that all students will have a better edition to use. In addition, we are grateful to Ms. Qing Gao of the Harvard-Yenching Library for her thorough and professional help in making the final corrections.

While we have made a concerted effort to make this edition as accurate as possible, we welcome user input and recommendations as part of our commitment to improving our products.

Publisher's Note to the First Edition

The Cheng & Tsui Company is pleased to make available the first two volumes of the traditional (or full) character edition of the *Practical Chinese Reader,* the highly successful introductory Chinese language textbook compiled by the Beijing Language Institute and published by the Commercial Press.

The Beijing Language Institute, the leading institution teaching Chinese as a foreign language in the People's Republic of China, produces many significant and valuable language texts. Unfortunately, many of these texts have not been widely known or available in the West. The *C&T Asian Language Series* is designed to publish and widely distribute quality language texts as they are completed by teachers at leading educational institutions, such as the Bejiing Language Institute.

While the substantive text in this Traditional Character Edition is unchanged, we have made some editorial judgments, so that the book does not correspond page for page to the original Simplified Character Edition. Specifically, we give all explanatory material in English only; non-essential pictures are not always included or in the same place as in the simplified edition; and we have deleted the "Table of Stroke Order of Chinese Charactes" in each lesson and compiled them in a separate volume entitled *Practical Chinese Reader I and II: Writing Workbook,* in which students can practice writing.

Additionally, we have also published the supplements *Practical Chinese Reader I: Patterns and Exercises* and *Practical Chinese Reader II: Patterns and Exercises* to provide the grammatical reinforcement lacking in the primary texts.

We would like to note that were it not for the tireless efforts of Professor Shou-hsin Teng, the Chief Editor of our Editorial Board, this Traditional Character Edition of *Practical Chinese Reader* might never have been published, and certainly not in its present complete and attractively typeset form.

Finally, we sincerely invite readers' comments and suggestions concerning the publications in this series. If you have comments or suggestions, please contact the following members of the Editorial Board:

Professor Shou-hsin Teng, Chief Editor
3 Coach Lane, Amherst, MA 01002

Professor Dana Scott Bourgerie
Asian and Near Eastern Languages,
Brigham Young University, Provo, UT 84602

Professor Samuel Cheung
Division of the Humanities, Hong Kong University of
Science and Technology, Hong Kong

Professor Ying-che Li
Dept. of East Asian Languages, University of Hawaii,
Honolulu, HI 96822

Professor Timothy Light
Dept. of Religion, Western Michigan University,
Kalamazoo, MI 49008

Introduction

Practical Chinese Reader is designed for foreign learners of elementary Chinese, primarily in a classroom setting, although it may also be used as a self-study course of modern Mandarin Chinese.

The fifty lessons in Books I and II aim to teach the communication of everyday Chinese and to lay a solid foundation for further Chinese language studies. These goals are accomplished by means of pattern substitution, functional item drills, grammatical analysis and various types of multiple-purpose exercises.

This course is devised on the following principles:

1. The texts are prepared in current, standard, and idiomatic modern Chinese, as spoken by native speakers. Priority is given to the most essential language items that the learner will need to express himself in everyday Chinese conversation.

2. This course aims not only to teach the learner speech forms, but more importantly enables the learner to use speech forms freely in specific situations. The situations involve two foreign students, Palanka and Gubo, who studied Chinese first in their country and then in China, where they make friends with native speakers. In Book I, Palanka and Gubo are represented as living in another part of the world, with the goal of enabling the learner to use Chinese in his own country.

3. Since it is important for adult learners to observe the basic rules of pronunciation and grammar, the textbook emphasizes language practice. Care has also been taken to include information respecting Chinese phonetics and grammar.

4. In order to ensure good results in language study, it is necessary for the learner to have some understanding of China's culture and history and present-day condition. For this purpose, background information on Chinese society, history, scenic spots, historical sites, local customs and conditions has been incorporated wherever possible. This information has been primarily incorporated into Book II.

5. The vocabulary, sentence patterns and their extensions, grammar, texts, reading texts and exercises in each lesson are arranged to ensure the recurrence of basic vocabulary and sentence patterns.

Since student backgrounds vary greatly, the teacher is given considerable flexibility to adapt the book to the needs of actual learners. He may use the book in whole or only in part, or change the order of the presentation.

Guide to the Book:

Text: Most of the texts are written in dialogue format, which facilitates audio-lingual practice and provides an overall grounding in reading and writing elementary Chinese.

New Words: Apart from the required lexical items, an optional list of words and expressions is included in each lesson.

Notes: Following each text are a number of notes that explain difficult sentences and expressions, give additional explanations about grammar items already covered, and provide necessary background information. Although some difficult sentences may contain grammar items that are dealt with in later lessons, the students are merely required to understand these sentences.

Pronunciation Drills (included in Lessons 1-12) **and Pronunciation and Intonation:** Apart from their focal task of providing practice in conversation and basic sentence patterns, the first twelve lessons contain a concentrated dose of drills in pronunciation and tones, with an emphsasis on items that have proven difficult for foreign learners. This type of drill, which is meant to give the learner a reasonably good grounding in phonetics, continues through each lesson. Intonation drills are also added.

Conversation Practice (included in Lessons 1-12) **and Substitution and Extension:** The mechanical substitutional drills aim to give the learner a proficient but formal mastery of basic sentence patterns. These are followed by situational extension type drills, which are designed to enable the learner to use the sentence patterns with reasonable freedom.

Phonetics (included in Lessons 1-12) **and Grammar:** The phonetics and grammar items included in this book are not treated in a comprehensive and systematic manner, but are dealt with in a way that best solves the specific difficulties of the foreign learners. Due attention has also been given to peculiarities of the Chinese language. The short grammatical summary included in the revision lesson following each unit recapitulates the items that have been taught up to that point.

Reading Text: These texts are designed to ensure the recurrence of some of the vocabulary items and sentence patterns already taught, as well as to develop the students' reading comprehension and consecutive speaking and writing skills.

Exercises: The various types of exercises are designed to consolidate the main grammar items covered, including the vocabulary items dealt with in the notes. It is hoped that students will make full use of the illustrations for situational oral practice.

Characters: The "Table of Stroke-Order of Chinese Characters" in each lesson of the Simplified Character Edition has been deleted from this Traditional Charcter Edition. This information is compiled in a separate workbook entitled *Practical Chinese Reader I and II: Writing Workbook,* which allows students to practice writing.

We gratefully acknowledge the teachers of the Beijing Language Institute, who offered generous advice and assistance in the preparation of *Practical Chinese Reader* Book I and II. Teachers and students both at home and abroad are earnestly invited to offer criticisms and suggestions. This critique will be invaluable to the revision of these two volumes and the preparation of future volumes.

These books are translated into English by He Peihui, Xiong Wenhua and Mei Xiuxian, and illustrated by Jin Tingting and Zhang Zhizhong.

–Compilers
February 1981

PRACTICAL CHINESE READER
Book One
Traditional Character Edition

TABLE OF CONTENTS

Page

第 一 課

一、課 文

你　好

Pàlánkǎ:　Gǔbō, nǐ hǎo!
　　Gubo, 你好！

Gǔbō:　Nǐ hǎo, Pàlánkǎ!
　　你好，Palanka!

二、生　詞

1. 你　　　　　nǐ　　　　　　you (sing.)
2. 好　　　　　hǎo　　　　　good, well

專　名

1. Gǔbō　　　a personal name
2. Pàlánkǎ　　a personal name

(1, 2)

三、注釋 Notes

"你好！"

"How are you?" or "Good morning (good afternoon or good evening)."

"你好" is a common greeting. It may be used in the morning, in the afternoon or in the evening. The answer to it from the person addressed is also "你好".

四、語音練習與會話練習
Pronunciation Drills and Conversation Practice

(一)

Initials	b	p	g	k	h	l	n
Finals	a	o	i	u	ao		an

1. The four tones

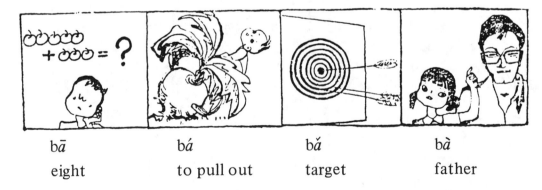

bā   bá   bǎ   bà
eight   to pull out target   father

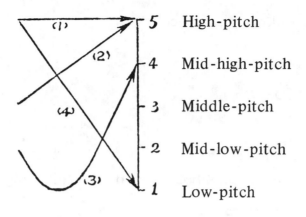

-:	1st tone		´:	2nd tone
˅:	3rd tone		ˋ:	4th tone

nī	ní	nǐ	nì	⎫
hāo	háo	hǎo	hào	⎬ nǐ hǎo

gū	gú	gǔ	gù	⎫
bō	bó	bǒ	bò	⎬ Gǔbō

pā	pá	(pǎ)	pà	⎫
(lān)	lán	lǎn	làn	⎬ Pàlánkǎ
kā	ká	kǎ	(kà)	⎭

2. Sound discrimination

bō – pō   lǐ – nǐ
pà – bà   lán – nán
gǔ – kǔ   hǔ – gǔ
kǎ – gǎ   hǎ – kǎ

3. Tone discrimination (1st tone and 4th tone)

bō – bò   kū – kù
pā – pà   gāo – gào
pī – pì   kān – kàn

4. Tone changes

3rd tone plus another 3rd tone → 2nd tone plus 3rd tone
nǐ hǎo → ní hǎo

5. Read out the following sentences
    Nǐ hǎo.
    Gǔbō, nǐ hǎo.
    Pàlánkǎ, nǐ hǎo.

(二)

Exchanging greetings

(1) Say as much as you can about each of the following pictures:

A: Nǐ hǎo.

B: _____:

A: _____:

B: Nǐ hǎo.

(2) Imagine yourselves to be Palanka and Gubo and greet each other

Gǔbō: Pàlánkǎ, nǐ hǎo!   Pàlánkǎ: Nǐ hǎo, Gǔbō.

Pàlánkǎ: _____ !   Gǔbō: _____ .

(3) Practise the greeting in pairs.

五、語音 Phonetics

1. Initials and finals

There are more than 400 basic syllables in the common speech of modern Chinese. A syllable in Chinese is usually composed of an initial,

(4, 5)   — 4 —

which is a consonant that begins the syllable, and a final, which covers the rest of the syllable. In the syllable "ba", for instance, "b" is an initial and "a" is a final.

The initial of a Chinese syllable is always a consonant. The final is a vowel, which may be a simple vowel (known as a "simple final", e.g. "a"), a compound vowel (known as a "compound final", e.g. "ao") or a vowel followed by a nasal consonant (known as a "nasal final", e.g. "an").

In modern Chinese, there are altogether 21 initials and 38 finals. A syllable can stand without an initial, but no syllable will do without a final.

2.　How to pronounce these initials and finals

Initials b[p] and g[k]

These are both unaspirated plosives, and they are voiceless consonants, i.e., the vocal cords do not vibrate in pronouncing them.

Initials p[p'] and k[k']

These are voiceless plosives, but they are aspirated, i.e., they are followed by a puff of suddenly released breath.

Compound final ao[au]

"ao" is produced by naturally moving the tongue from "a" in the direction of "o". The tongue-position for "a" in "ao" is a little more to the back than that for the simple vowel "a". "a" is pronounced both longer and louder than "o", which is pronounced much less distinctly, with the tongue a little higher than in the case of the simple vowel "a".

Nasal final an[an]

This is an alveolar nasal final, produced by pronouncing "a" first, with the tongue-position a little more to the front than in the case of the simple voel "a", then raising the tip of the tongue against the gum and lowering the soft palate at the same time to let the air out through the nasal cavity.

3.　Tones

Chinese is a language with different tones that are capable of differenciating meanings. A syllable, when pronounced in a different tone, has a different meaning even if it is composed of the same initial and final. In the Beijing dialect there are four basic tones, represented respectively by the following tone-graphs: "-" (the 1st tone), "ˊ" (the 2nd tone), "ˇ" (the 3rd tone) and "ˋ" (the 4th tone).

When a syllable contains a single vowel only, the tone-graph is placed directly above the vowel sound. (The dot over the vowel "i" should be dropped if the tone-graph is placed above it, as in "nǐ".) When the final of a syllable is composed of two or more vowels (that is, when it is a diphthong or triphthong), the tone-graph should be placed above the main vowel (namely the one pronounced with the mouth widest open), e.g. "hǎo".

4. Tone changes

A 3rd tone, when immediately followed by another 3rd tone, should be pronounced in the 2nd tone, but with the tone-graph "ˇ" remaining unchanged. "nǐ hǎo", for example, becomes "ní hǎo" in actual pronunciation.

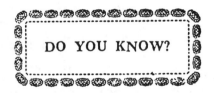

DO YOU KNOW?

The Chinese Language

What is usually referred to as Chinese is in fact the language of China's largest nationality, the Hans. It is the main language spoken in China and one of the world's major languages, ranking among the official as well as woking languages at the United Nations and other international organs.

The Chinese language is one of the oldest languages in the world, its earliest written records going as far back as more than 3,000 years ago. During this long period of time, Chinese has seen constant development, but its grammar, vocabulary and writing system have in the main retained their basic features. What we propose to teach in this textbook is what is known as "the common speech", the kind of modern Chinese with "the Beijing speech sounds as the standard sounds, the Northern dialect as the basic dialect and modern classic works written in the vernacular as its grammatical models".

你 好

第 二 課

一、課 文

你 好 嗎

Gǔbō: Nǐ hǎo ma?
你好嗎？

Pàlánkǎ: Wǒ hěn hǎo, nǐ ne?
我很好，你呢？

Gǔbō: Yě hěn hǎo.
也很好。

二、生 詞

1. 嗎　　　　ma　　　　an interrogative particle
2. 我　　　　wǒ　　　　I, me
3. 很　　　　hěn　　　　very
4. 呢　　　　ne　　　　a modal particle
5. 也　　　　yě　　　　also, too

(10, 11)　　　　　　　　　— 8 —

三、注釋 Notes

1. "你好嗎？"

   "How are you?"

   "你好嗎？" is also a common greeting, and one of the commonly used answers is "我很好".

2. "你呢？"

   "And (how are) you?"

3. "也很好。"

   "(I'm) very well, too."

   "也很好" is an elliptical sentence in which the subject "我" is omitted. In colloquial speech in Chinese, subjects of this kind are often omitted if the context leaves no room for misunderstanding. "我很好" in the text can also be further shortened to "很好".

四、語音練習與會話練習
Pronunciation Drills and Conversation Practice

(一)

Initial	m			
Finals	e	uo	ie	en

1. The four tones

nī	ní	nǐ	nì	
hāo	háo	hǎo	hào	} nǐ hǎo ma
mā	má	mǎ	mà	
wō	wó	wǒ	wò	
(nē)	né	(ně)	nè	– nǐ ne

(11, 12)

(hēn)   hén   hěn   hèn
yē   yé   yě   yè – yě hěn hāo

2. Sound discrimination

hé – hén   biē – piē
lè – liè   bèn – pèn
kǎn – kěn   gē – kē
mō – māo   guò – kuò

3. Tone changes

Half 3rd tone

Nǐ ne?

Hǎo ma?

Gǔbō

A 3rd tone changing into a 2nd tone

Nǐ   hǎo.   (Ní hǎo.)
Hěn   hǎo.   (Hén hǎo.)
Wǒ   hěn hǎo.   (Wó   hén hǎo.)
Yě   hǎo.   (Yé hǎo.)
Yě   hěn hǎo.   (Yé hén hǎo.)

māo

(二)

Exchanging greetings

(1) A: Nǐ hǎo ma?
     B: _____ , _____?
     A: Yě hěn hǎo.

(2) A: Nǐ hǎo ma?
     B: _____ :
     A: Gǔbō ne?
     B: _____ :

(3) A: Gǔbō hǎo ma?
     B: _____ :

A: Pàlánkǎ ne?

B: _____ :

五、語音 Phonetics

1. How to pronounce these finals

Simple final e[ɤ]

e[ɤ] is a back, unrounded vowel, formed with the tongue in a mid-high position. It is produced by pronouncing "o" first, then changing from lip rounding to lip spreading, but with the tongue-position remaining the same.

Compound final ie[iɛ]

The "e" in "ie" is a simple final "ê" [ɛ] which is seldom used alone (with the mouth half-open, the corners of the mouth spread wide, the tip of the tongue against the back of the lower teeth). "ie" is produced by pronouncing "i" is first, then promptly sliding in the direction of "ê", which is pronounced louder and longer than "I".

Compound final uo[uo]

It is produced by pronouncing "u" first, then promptly sliding in the direction of "o", which is pronounced louder and longer than "u".

2. Neutral tone

In the Chinese common speech there are a number of syllables which are unstressed and take a feeble tone. This is known as the neutral tone which is shown by the absence of a tone-graph, as in "Nǐ ne?" and "Hǎo ma?".

3. Half 3rd tone

A 3rd tone, when followed by a 1st, 2nd or 4th tone or most neutral tones, usually becomes a half 3rd tone, that is, the tone that only falls but does not rise. The 3rd tone is seldom used in full unless it occurs as an independent tone or when followed by a long pause. In most cases it is changed into a half 3rd tone, but with its tone-graph unchanged.

4. Rules of phonetic spelling

At the beginning of a syllable, "i" is written as "y", e.g. "ie→ye". "i" is written as "yi" when it forms a syllable all by itself, e.g. "yī".

At the beginning of a syllable, "u" is written as "w", e.g. "uo→wo". "u" is written as "wu" when it forms a syllable all by itself, e.g. "wǔ".

六、語法 Grammar

1. The word order in a Chinese sentence

The Chinese language is characterized by its total lack of inflectional endings employed by other languages to express person, tense, gender, number and case. Word order, or the arrangement of words, in a sentence, is thus an extremely important means in expressing the various grammatical relationships.

A Chinese sentence usually begins with the subject followed by the predicate. E.g.

你好。

我很好。

(我)也很好。

In the three sentences above, " 你 " and " 我 " are the subjects while " 好 " is the main element of the predicates. The adverbs " 也 " and " 好 " function as adverbial adjuncts to qualify the predicative adjective " 好 ". In Chinese, an adverb must precede what it qualifies (usually a verb or an adjective).

2. Questions with the interrogative particle " 嗎 "

When the interrogative particle " 嗎 " is added at the end of a declarative sentence, it becomes a general question. The word order of such a ques-

(15, 16)

tion is exactly the same as that of the answer to it. E.g.

你好。

你好嗎?

我很好。

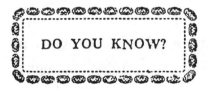

DO YOU KNOW?

Chinese Characters

Chinese, which is formed of characters, is among the world's oldest written languages. Generally speaking, each character stands for a meaningful syllable. The total number of Chinese characters is estimated at more than 50,000 of which only 5,000—8,000 are in common use. Of these merely 3,000 are used for everyday purposes.

甲骨文	☉	D	↯	⌇	⌵	𤣥
钟鼎文	⊖	⅊	⌄	⌇	羊	象
篆书	⊖	ⅅ	火	水	羊	象
隶书	日	月	火	水	羊	马
楷书	日	月	火	水	羊	马

(17, 18)

The Chinese characters in use today developed from the pictographs cut on oracle bones dating from over 3,000 years ago and the pictographs found on ancient bronze vessels dating a little later. In the course of their history of development, Chinese characters evolved from pictographs into characters formed of strokes, with their structures very much simpler. Most of the present-day Chinese characters are known as pictophonetic characters, each formed of two elements, with one indicating the meaning and the other the sound.

Chinese characters have made great contributions to the long history of the Chinese nation and Chinese culture, and Chinese calligraphy is a highly developed art. But Chinese characters have serious drawbacks. It is very difficult to learn, to read and to write and still more difficult to memorize. Reforms should be carried out to make the characters easier.

你　好　嗎

第 三 課

一、課 文

你 忙 嗎

Gubo: Nǐ máng ma?
你忙嗎？

Palanka: (Wǒ) bù máng.
（我）不忙。

Gubo: Nǐ gēge hǎo ma?
你哥哥好嗎？

Palanka: Tā hěn hǎo.
他很好。

Nǐ gēge, nǐ dìdi hǎo ma?
你哥哥、你弟弟好嗎？

Gubo: Tāmen dōu hěn hǎo.
他們都很好。

二、生　詞

1. 忙　　　　máng　　　　busy
2. 不　　　　bù　　　　　not, no
3. 哥哥　　　gēge　　　　elder brother
4. 他　　　　tā　　　　　he, him
5. 弟弟　　　dìdi　　　　younger brother
6. 他們　　　tāmen　　　they, them
7. 都　　　　dōu　　　　all

三、注釋 Notes

1. "你哥哥好嗎?"

In Chinese, a personal pronoun can be put immediately before nouns indicating family relationships as an attributive to show possession, e.g. "你弟弟", "我哥哥" and "他弟弟" etc.

2. "他們都很好。"

The adverb "都" must follow the subject but precede the predicative verb or predicative adjective. It is never found before the subject and it is wrong to say "都他們很好".

四、語音練習與會話練習
Pronunciation Drills and Conversation Practice

(一)

Initials	d	t
Finals	ou	*ang*

1. The four tones

gē   gé   gě   gè   — gēge
dī   dí   dǐ   dì   — dìdi
tā   tá   tǎ   tà   ⎫
mēn   mén   (měn)   mèn ⎬ tāmen
                             ⎭

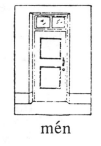

mén

(māng) máng   mǎng   (màng) — bù máng
dōu   dóu   dǒu   dòu   — dōu hěn hǎo

2. Sound discrimination

dì — tì   kē — gē

— 17 —

dā — tā   kǒu – gǒu
bǎng – pǎng   tōu – dōu
bù   – pù   hěn – kěn

3. Tone discrimination (4th tone and 2nd tone)

dì – dí   mò – mó
bù – bú   tàng – táng
mèn – mén   hòu – hóu

4. Tone changes—half 3rd tone

nǐ gēge   wǒ gēge
nǐ dìdi   wǒ dìdi
Nǐ máng ma?   Wǒ bù máng.

5. The four tones and neutral tone

Nǐ gēge hǎo ma?   Tā gēge máng ma?
Tā dìdi hǎo ma?   Nǐ dìdi máng ma?
Tāmen hǎo ma?   Tāmen máng ma?

(一)

Exchanging greetings

(1) A: Nǐ hǎo ma?
    B: _____ :
    A: Nǐ gēge hǎo ma?
    B: _____ :
    A: Tā máng ma?
    B: _____ :
    A: Nǐmen dōu máng ma?
    B: _____ :

(2) A: Nǐ dìdi máng ma?
    B: _____ :
    A: Tā hǎo ma?
    B: _____ :

(23)

A: Nǐ dìdi yě hǎo ma?

B: _____ :

A: Tāmen dōu hǎo ma?

B: _____ :

(3) A: Nǐ máng ma?

B: _____ :

A: Pàlánkǎ máng ma?

B: _____ :

A: Pàlánkǎ hǎo ma?

B: _____ :

(4) A: Nǐ hǎo!

B: _____ !

A: Nǐ máng ma?

B: _____ : _____ ?

A: Yě bù máng.

A: _____ ?

B: Hěn máng. Nǐ ne?

A: _____ :

A: Gǔbō máng ma?

B: _____ :

A: Pàlánkǎ ne?

B: _____ :

(5) A: Tā gēge hǎo ma?

B: _____ :

A: Tā dìdi ne?

B: _____ :

五、語音 Phonetics

1. How to pronounce these finals

Compound final ou[əu]

In pronouncing the "o" in "ou", the lips are not so rounded as in the case of the simple final "o". Moreover, "o" is pronounced long and loud whereas "u" is pronounced light, short and somewhat indistinct with the lips a little laxer than for the simple final "u".

Nasal final *ang*[aŋ]

ang[aŋ] is a velar nasal final. It is produced by pronouncing "*a*" first, with the tongue-position a little more to the back, then promptly retracting the tongue backward, with the root of the tongue against the soft palate, and lowering the soft palate at the same time to let the air out through the nasal cavity.

2. The aspirated and unaspirated

The unaspirated "b" and aspirated "p" are pronounced in exactly the same manner as regards tongue-positions. So are "d"[t] and "t"[t‘], "c" and "k" (and "zh" and "ch", "j" and "q" and "z" and "c" to be introduced in later lessons): The only difference is that, in pronouncing the aspirated "p, t, k (and ch, q and c as well)", the air is puffed out strongly, whereas with the unaspirated "b, d, *g* (and zh, j and z)" the air is let out with a pop through the lips. Learners can put a small piece of paper in front of the mouth to see if the puffing is properly done or not.

Note that in Chinese, the unaspirated are also voiceless consonants. The vocal cords do not vibrate when they are pronounced.

六、語法 Grammar

Sentences with an adjectival predicate

A sentence in which the main element of the predicate is an adjective is known as a sentence with an adjectival predicate. E.g.

我很好。

他很忙。

他們都很好。

Sentences of this kind are made negative by putting the adverb " 不 " before the predicative adjective, as in " 我不忙 ".

*

Nouns or pronouns	Adverbs	Adjectives	Particle
我 你 我	很 不	好。 好 忙。	嗎?

---

*Tables in the grammar sections of this book include only those sentence patterns dealt with in the initial stage.

第 四 課

一、課 文

這是我朋友

Palanka: Zhè shì wǒ bàba.
這是我爸爸。

Zhè shì wǒ māma.
這是我媽媽。

Zhè shì wǒ péngyou—Gǔbō.
這是我朋友 —Gǔbō.

Gubo: Nǐmen hǎo!
你們好!

Bàba Mǎma : Nǐ hǎo!
你好!

二、生 詞

1.這   zhè   this

(29, 30)

— 22 —

2.是	shì	to be
3.朋友	péngyou	friend
4.爸爸	bàba	father
5.媽媽	māma	mother
6.你們	nǐmen	you (pl.)

— 23 —

三、注釋 Notes

1. "這是我爸爸。"

"This is my father."

The expression "這是…" is usually used to introduce one person to another, and the expression "我是…" is used when one introduces oneself. "是" in both expressions is pronounced light.

2. "你們好。"

"你們好" is used to greet more than one person.

四、語音練習與會話練習
Pronunciation Drills and Conversation Practice

(一)

Initials	zh	sh	
Finals	-i[ʅ]	iou(-iu)	eng

1. The four tones and neutral tone

zhē	zhé	zhě	zhè
shī	shí	shǐ	shì	} zhè shì
bā	bá	bǎ	bà — bàba
mā	má	mǎ	mà — māma
pēng	péng	pěng	pèng
yōu	yóu	yǒu	yòu	} péngyou

2. Sound discrimination

zhēn – zhēng   dàng – dèng

shuō – shōu   zhǐ – zhě

liú – lóu   shé – shí

3. Tone discrimination (2nd tone and 1st tone)

péng — pēng   shé — shē

zhí — zhī   zhóu — zhōu

shéng — shēng   shén — shēn

4. Tone changes—half 3rd tone

wǒ māma	nǐ māma
wǒ gēge	nǐ gēge
wǒ péngyou	nǐ péngyou
wǒ dìdi	nǐ dìdi
wǒ bàba	nǐ bàba
wǒmen	nǐmen
haǒ ma	nǐ ne

5. Read out the following phrases:

tā māma	tā péngyou
tā bàba	tā hǎo

(二)

1. Identifying people or objects

Gubo: Zhè   shì   wǒ   bàba,
                zhè   shì   wǒ   māma.
Palanka: Zhè   shì   tā   bàba,
                zhè   shì   tā   māma.

Gubo: _____ ,
           _____ :

Palanka: _____ ,
           _____ :

(32, 33)

A: _____ :

B: _____ :

2. Introducing one person to another
    A: Zhè shì _____ .
       Zhè shì _____ :
    B: Nǐ hǎo!
    C: Nǐ hǎo!

3. Introducing oneself
    A: Nǐ hǎo, wǒ shì _____ .
    B: Nǐ hǎo, wǒ shì _____ :

4. Greeting each other

    (1)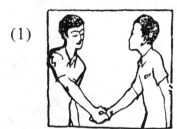
    A: _____ :

    B: _____ :

    A: _____ :

    B.C.D: _____ :

    (2) Nǐ bàba máng ma?
         Wǒ bàba hěn máng.

māma
péngyou

(3) A: Nǐ bàba hǎo ma?

     B: Tā hěn hǎo.

     A: Nǐ māma ne?

     B: Tā yě hěn hǎo.

(4) A: Nǐ máng ma?

     B: Wǒ bù máng.

     A: Nǐ péngyou máng ma?

     B: Tā _____ bù máng.

     A: Nǐ gēge, nǐ dìdi ne?

     B: Tāmen _____ bù máng.

gēge,	dìdi
māma,	péngyou
dìdi,	péngyou

五、語音 Phonetics

How to pronounce these initials and finals

Initial zh[tʂ]

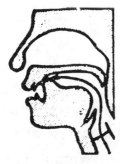

The initial zh[tʂ] is a blade-palatal, unaspirated voiceless affricate. It is produced by curling the tip of the tongue and raising it against the front part of the hard palate, allowing a narrow opening between the tongue-tip and the hard palate for the air to squeeze out. The vocal cords do not vibrate in pronouncing it.

Initial sh[ʂ]

The initial sh[ʂ] is a blade-palatal voiceless fricative. It is produced by curling the tip of the tongue and raising it to the hard palate, leaving a narrow opening between them to allow the air to squeeze out through it. The vocal cords do not vibrate in pronouncing it.

(34, 35)

Simple final -i [ʃ]

The letter "i" is used to stand for the blade-palatale vowel [ʃ] after the initial "sh, zh" (and "ch" and "r" to be introduced in the next two lessons). In order to distinguish the simple final "i[ʃ]" from the simple final "i[i]", "i[ʃ]" is written as "−i" when it stands alone. In pronouncing such syllables as "zhi" and "chi", the tongue is kept still, and care must be taken not to pronounce it as the simple final "i[i]" which is never found after "zh, ch, sh" or "r".

Compound final iou[iəu]

The compound final "iou[iəu]" is produced by first lowering the tongue from the position of "i" to that for "o", then raising the tongue from the position of "o" to that of "u". The compound final "iou" is written as "iu" when it comes after an initial and the tone-graph is placed on the last element, e.g. "liù".

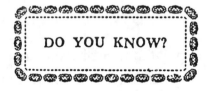

DO YOU KNOW?

Scheme for the Chinese Phonetic Alphabet

"The Scheme for the Chinese Phonetic Alphabet", which was adopted at the First Plenary Session of the First National People's Congress of the People's Republic of China on February 21, 1958, is a set of symbols used to transliterate Chinese characters and combine the speech sounds of the common speech into syllables. The scheme makes use of the Latin alphabet, modified to meet the needs of the Chinese language. The scheme, which will form the foundation for the creation of a Chinese alphabetic system of writing, is being used throughout the country to facilitate the learning of Chinese characters, help unify pronunciation and popularize the common speech. The scheme has for years been used among foreign learners of Chinese as well and has been found much useful and helpful.

(36, 37, 38)

第 五 課

一、課 文

你媽媽是大夫嗎

Gubo:　　Zhè shì nǐ de chē ma?
這是你的車嗎？

Palanka:　Zhè bú shì wǒ de chē,
這不是我的車，

　　　　　Zhè shì wǒ māma de chē.
這是我媽媽的車。

Gubo:　　Nà shì tā de shū ma?
那是她的書嗎？

Palanka:　Nà shì tā de shū.
那是她的書。

Gubo:　　Nǐ māma shì dàifu ma?
你媽媽是大夫嗎？

Palanka:　Shì, tā shì dàifu.

　　　　是，她是大夫。

二、生　詞

1.大夫	dàifu	doctor
2.的	de	a structural particle
3.車	chē	vehicle
4.那	nà	that
5.她	tā	she, her
6.書	shū	book

補　充　詞

1.　bào　　　　newspaper

2.　zhǐ　　　　paper

3.　chǐ　　　　ruler

4.　bǐ　　　　pen, pencil, writing brush

三、注釋 Notes

1. "這是你的車嗎"

    "Is this your car?"

    "車" is a general term for land vehicles of all kinds. In different context, it may refer to a motor-car, a train or a bicycle. In the present lesson "車" refers to a sedan.

2. "那是她的書嗎？"

    "Is that her book?"

In Chinese, there are two different characters for the singular third person pronoun "ta": one is "他" denoting a male person, the other is "她" denoting a female person. Both "他" and "她" are sounded exactly the same.

四、語音練習與會話練習
Pronunciation Drills and Conversation Practice

(一)

Initials	(zh)	ch	(sh)	f
Final	ai			

1. The four tones

chē	ché	chě	chè
bū	bú	bǔ	bù — bú shì
nā	ná	nǎ	nà
shū	shú	shǔ	shù
dāi	dái	dǎi	dài
fū	fú	fǔ	fù

⎫
⎬ dàifu
⎭

2. Sound discrimination

zhǐ	– chǐ		bǐ	– pǐ
bào	– pào		gāi	– kāi
zhái	– chái		chóu	– shóu

3. Tone discrimination (4th tone and 1st tone)

chè	– chē		chì	– chī
dài	– dāi		fèn	– fēn
shù	– shū		chàng	– chāng

4. Tone changes – half 3rd tone and neutral tone

nǐ de shū		nǐmen de chē	
wǒ de shū		wǒmen de chē	
tā de shū		tāmen de chē	

5. Read out the following sentences:

(1) A: Nǐ gēge shì dàifu ma?

B: Wǒ gēge bú shì dàifu,
   wǒ péngyou shì dàifu.

(2) A: Nà shì nǐ de shū ma?

B: Nà bú shì wǒ de shū,
   nà shì wǒ dìdi de shū.

(二)

1. Identifying people or objects

(1) A: Zhè shì shū ma?

B: _____ :

A: Nà shì bǐ ma?

B: _____ :

A: Nà shì bào ma?

B: _____ :

(2) A: Zhè shì nǐ de chē ma?
    B: Zhè bú shì wǒ de chē.
        Zhè shì tā de chē.

shū	bǐ
chǐ	zhǐ

(3) A: Nà shì tā gēge ma?
    B: Nà bú shì tā gēge.
        Nà shì tā péngyou.

dìdi
bàba

(4) A: Tā shì nǐ péngyou ma?
    B: Tā bú shì wǒ péngyou.
        Tā shì wǒ māma de péngyou.

gēge
dìdi
bàba

2. Asking about someone's occupation
   A: Nǐ shì dàifu ma?
   B: Shì, wǒ shì dàifu.

tā	tāmen
nǐmen	nǐ bàba

五、語音 Phonetics

1. How to pronounce the initial and final

Initial ch[tʂ']

The initial "ch[tʂ']" is the correspondent aspirated to the unaspirated "zh".

Compound final ai[ai]

The compound final "ai[ai]" is produced by first articulating "a", a front vowel pronounced long and loud with the tongue-position a little more to the front than for "a" as an independent final, then gliding in the direction of "i" which is pronounced light, short and somewhat indistinct.

2. Tones of "不"

"不" is pronounced in the 4th tone when it stands by itself or precedes a 1st, 2nd or 3rd tone, but is pronounced in the 2nd tone when it precedes another 4th tone (or a neutral tone that is originally a 4th tone), e.g. "bù máng", "bù hǎo", "bú shì".

六、語法 Grammar

1. Sentence type (1)

A sentence in which the predicate is made up of the verb "是" and one other word or phrase is known as a "是" sentence. In a "是" sentence, the verb "是" is usually pronounced light. Such a sentence is made negative by putting "不" in front of "是".

Nouns or pronouns	Adverb	Verb "是"	Nouns or pronouns	Particle
這 這 那	不	是 是 是	你的車 我的車。 她的書。	嗎?

2. Attributives showing possession

When a noun or a pronoun is used attributively to show possession, it must take after it the structural particle "的", as in "你的車", "她的書" and "媽媽的車".

When a personal pronoun is used attributively to show possession, it is used without "的" if the qualified word denotes a family relationship or a unit of which the speaker (or the person spoken to or of) is a member, e.g. "我爸爸", "你哥哥".

In Chinese, an attributive must precede what it qualifies.

第 六 課

一、課 文

他 是 哪 國 人

Palanka:　Nà shì shéi?
　　　　　那是誰？

Gubo:　　Nà shì wǒmen lǎoshī.
　　　　　那是我們老師。

Palanka:　Tā shì nǎ guó rén?
　　　　　他是哪國人？

Gubo:　　Tā shì Zhōngguó rén.
　　　　　他是 Zhōngguó 人。

Palanka:　Tā shì Hànyǔ lǎoshī ma?
　　　　　他是漢語老師嗎？

Gubo:　　Tā shì Hànyǔ lǎoshī.
　　　　　他是漢語老師。

　　　　　　　(48, 49)

二、生 詞

1. 哪　　　　nǎ　　　　which
2. 國　　　　guó　　　　country
3. 人　　　　rén　　　　person
4. 誰　　　　shéi　　　　who
5. 我們　　　wǒmen　　　we, us
6. 老師　　　lǎoshī　　　teacher
7. 漢語　　　Hànyǔ　　　Chinese (language)

專　名

Zhōngguó　　　　　　China

補　充　詞

1. Déguó　　　　Germany
2. Fǎguó　　　　France
3. Měiguó　　　　the United States of America
4. Mǎlǐ　　　　Mali
5. Rìběn　　　　Japan

三、注釋 Notes

1. "那是誰？"

   "Who is that person?"

2. "他是哪國人？"

   "What's his nationality?"

3. "他是 Zhongguo 人。"

   "He is a Chinese."

To express the idea of "a certain person of a certain nationality", Chinese requires the addition of the word "人" to the name of the country.

4. "他是漢語老師嗎？"

   "Is he a teacher of Chinese?"

"漢語老師" means "a teacher who teaches Chinese".

四、語音練習與會話練習
Pronunciation Drills and Conversation Practice

(一)

```
Initials    (zh   ch   sh)        r
Finals        ü    ei   ong
```

1. The four tones

zhōng	zhóng	zhǒng	zhòng	⎤
guō	guó	guǒ	guò	⎬ Zhōngguó rén
(rēn)	rén	rěn	rèn	⎦
hān	hán	hǎn	hàn	⎫
yū	yú	yǔ	yù	⎬ Hànyǔ
lāo	láo	lǎo	lào	— lǎoshī

— 37 —

2. Sound discrimination

bēi — pēi

lái — léi

rǎo — shǎo

nǚ — nǔ

lǜ — lù

róng — réng

zhì — chì — shì — rì

zhè — chè — shè — rè

3. Tone discrimination (1st tone and 2nd tone)

guō — guó   tōng — tóng

rāng — ráng   fēi — féi

chōng — chóng   yū — yú

4. Tone changes — half 3rd tone and neutral tone.

wǒmen lǎoshī   wǒ gēge

nǐmen lǎoshī   nǐ dìdi

tāmen lǎoshī   tā péngyou

5. Read out the following words and phrases:

nǎ guó rén   Měiguó rén

Déguó reń   Mǎlǐ rén

Fǎguó rén   Rìběn rén

Zhōngguó rén

(二)

1. Identifying people or objects

(1)

A: Tā shì shéi?   A: Tā shì shéi?

B: _____ :   B: _____ :

A: Tā shì shéi?　　　　A: Tā shì shéi?

B: _____ :　　　B: _____ :

(2) A: Nà shì shéi?

　　B: Nà shì <u>wǒmen</u> lǎoshī.

nǐmen　　tāmen

Hànyǔ　　Zhōngguó

2. Asking about nationalities

(1)

A: Tā shì nǎ guó rén?　　A: _____ ?

B: _____ .　　　　B: Tā shì Rìběn rén.

A: Tā shì nǎ guó rén?　　A: Tā shì nǎ guó rén?

B: _____ .　　　　B: _____ :

　　　　(53, 54)

(2)　A:　Nǐ hǎo.

　　　　B:　Nǐ hǎo.

　　　　A:　Nǐ shì nǎ guó rén?

　　　　B:　Wǒ shì ＿＿＿＿ rén. Nǐ ne?

　　　　A:　Wǒ shì ＿＿＿＿ rén.

(3)　A:　Nǐ shì nǎ guó rén?

　　　　B:　Wǒ shì ＿＿＿＿ rén.

　　　　A:　Tā yě shì ＿＿＿＿ rén ma?

　　　　B:　Tā yě shì ＿＿＿＿ rén.

　　　　A:　Nǐmen dōu shì ＿＿＿＿ rén ma?

　　　　B:　Wǒmen dōu shì ＿＿＿＿ rén.

五、語音 Phonetics

1.　How to pronounce these initial and finals

Initial r[ʐ]

The initial "r[ʐ]" is a voiced fricative, pronounced in the same way as "sh", but with a very slight friction. The vocal cords vibrate.

Simple final ü[y]

The simple final "ü[y]" is produced by first articulating "i", then rounding and protruding the lips as much as possible, leaving a very small opening, but with the tongue kept still.

Compound final ei[ei]

The "e" in "ei" is pronounced as [e]. "e" is pronounced both long and loud whereas "i" is pronounced light, short and indistinct.

Nasal final ong[uŋ]

The nasal final "ong[uŋ]" is produced by first pronouncing "o", with the opening of the mouth somewhat smaller than in the case of the simple vowel "o" but about the same as for "u", then promptly retracting the tongue backward to press the back of the tongue against the soft palate and lowering the soft palate at the same time to let the air out through the nasal cavity.

2. Rules of phonetic spelling

When forming a syllable by itself or when occurring at the beginning of a syllable, "ü" is written as "yu", as in "Hànyǔ".

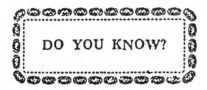
DO YOU KNOW?

China's Dialect Areas

The Chinese language has eight major dialects. The eight dialect areas are: North China (for the Northern dialect), Jiangsu-Zhejiang (for the Wu dialect), Hunan (for the Hunan dialect), Jiangxi (for the Jiangxi dialect), Kejia (for the Kejia dialect, a form of Chinese spoken by descendants of northerners who moved to Guangdong and nearby provinces centuries ago), northern Fujian (for the northern Fujian dialect), southern Fujian (for the southern Fujian dialect) and Guangdong (for the Yue, another name of Guangdong Province, dialect). Of all the Chinese-speaking population, about 70% speak the Northern dialect, which is the reason why it has been made the basis of the common speech.

The vocabulary and grammar are basically the same in all the dialects, the chief difference being in pronunciation. In order to remove barriers caused by dialectal differences and to facilitate and bring about a further political, cultural and economic development, a nation-wide campaign has been started to popularize the common speech.

第 七 課

一、課 文

這是什麼地圖

Zhè shì shéi de dìtú?
這是誰的地圖？

Zhè shì Gǔbō de dìtú.
這是 Gǔbō 的地圖。

Zhè shì shénme dìtú?
這是什麼地圖？

Zhè shì Zhōngguó dìtú.
這是 Zhōngguó 地圖。

Nǐ kàn, zhè shì Běijīng, nà shì Shànghǎi.
你看，這是 Běijīng ，那是 Shànghǎi 。

Zhè shì Cháng Jiāng ma?
這是 Cháng Jiāng 嗎？

Bú shì, zhè shì Huáng Hé, nà shì Cháng Jiāng.
不是，這是 Huáng Hé ，那是　Cháng Jiāng 。

Zhè shì shénme?
這是什麼？

Zhè shì Chángchéng.
這是Chángchéng。

二、生　詞

1.什麼　　　　shénme　　　　what

2.地圖　　　　dìtú　　　　map

3.看　　　　kàn　　　　to see, to look, to have a look, to read, to watch

專　名

1. Běijīng　　　Beijing

2. Shànghǎi　　　Shanghai

3. Cháng Jiāng　　the Changjiang (Yangtz) River

4. Huáng Hé　　the Huanghe (Yellow) River

5. Chángchéng　　the Great Wall

補　充　詞

1. shìjiè — world

2. Oū Zhōu — Europe

3. Fēi Zhōu — Africa

4. Dàyáng Zhōu — Oceania

5. Nán Měi Zhōu — South America

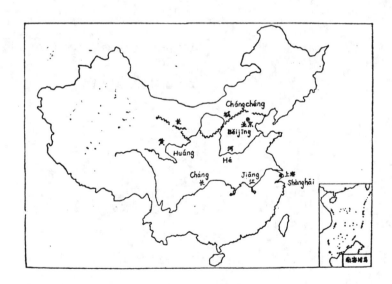

三、注釋 Notes

1. "這是誰的地圖？"
   "Whose map is this?"
2. "這是什麼地圖？"
   "What map is this?"
3. "你看。"
   "Look (you)."

四、語音練習與會話練習
Pronunciation Drills and Conversation Practice

(一)

```
Initial      ·j
Finals      ing      iang      uang
```

1. The four tones
   jīng   jíng   jǐng   jìng   — Běijīng
   jiāng   jiáng   jiǎng   jiàng — Cháng Jiāng
   huāng   huáng   huǎng   huàng — Huáng Hé
   chāng   cháng   chǎng   chàng — Chángchéng
   shēn   shén   shěn   shèn   — shénme

2. Sound discrimination
   bīng — pīng   láng — liáng
   zhuāng — chuāng   rén — réng
   bǎo — pǎo   dōu — diū
   kōng — gōng   nán — náng
   tiē — diē   yǔ — wǔ
   guò — kuò   máng — méng

3. Tone discrimination (2nd tone and 3rd tone)

chuáng – chuǎng   hái – hǎi
fáng – fǎng   méi – měi
yáng – yǎng   jié – jiě

4. Tone changes

(1) nǐ   hǎo   (3) nǐ   de   chē
     hěn   hǎo   wǒ   de   dìtú
     yě   hǎo

(2) nǐ   dìdi   (4) nǎ   guó rén
     wǒ   péngyou   Fǎguó   rén
     wǒmen lǎoshī   Měiguó   rén
     nǐmen lǎoshī

(二)

1. Identifying people or objects

(1)

 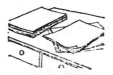

A: Zhè shì shénme?   A: Nà shì shénme?
B: Zhè shì _____ :   B: Nà shì _____ :

(61, 62)   — 46 —

(2) A: Zhè shì shéi de chē?
     B: Zhè shì wǒ de chē.

tā	dàifu
lǎoshī	tā péngyou

(3) A: Nà shì shénme dìtú?
     B: Nà shì Zhōngguó dìtú.

Běijīng	Fēi Zhōu
shìjiè	Dàyáng Zhōu
Ōu Zhōu	Nán Měi Zhōu

2. Asking about occupations and nationalities
   (1) Answer the following questions:
        Pàlánkǎ shì shéi?
        Pàlánkǎ de māma shì lǎoshī ma?
        Nà shì Pàlánkǎ de chē ma?
        Nà shì shéi de chē?
        Tā shì lǎoshī ma?
        Shéi shì nǐmen lǎoshī?
        Hànyǔ lǎoshī shì Měiguó rén ma?
        Hànyǔ lǎoshī shì nǎ guó rén?
   (2) Read out the following dialogue:
        A: Nǐ máng ma?
        B: Bù máng, nǐ ne?
        A: Wǒ hěn máng. Nǐ bàba, māma hǎo ma?
        B: Tāmen dōu hěn hǎo.
        A: Nà shì shéi?
        B: Nà shì Pàlánkǎ de bàba.
        A: Tā yě shì dàifu ma?
        B: Bú shì, tā shì lǎoshī.
        A: Tā shì shéi?
        B: Tā shì Gǔbō de lǎoshī.
        A: Tā shì Zhōngguó rén ma?
        B: Shì, tā shì Zhōngguó rén.

(3) Make up dialogues on each of the following pictures, using the words given in brackets:

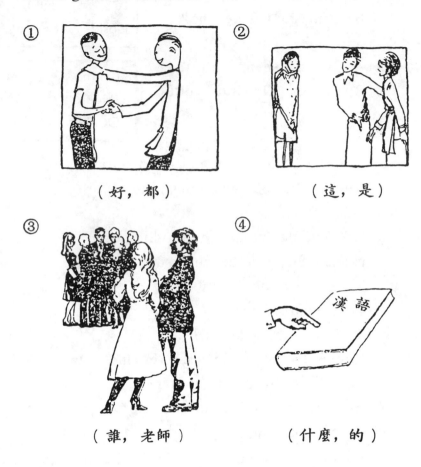

① （好，都）

② （這，是）

③ （誰，老師）

④ （什麼，的）

五、語音 Phonetics

How to pronounce the initial

Initial j[tɕ]

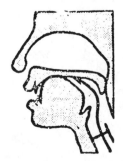

The initial j[tɕ] is produced by first raising the front of the tongue to the hard palate and pressing the tip of the tongue against the back of the lower teeth, then loosing the tongue to let the air squeeze out through the channel between the tongue and hard palate. The vocal cords do not vibrate in pronouncing this sound.

六、語法 Grammar

1. Questions with an interrogative pronoun

In Chinese, a question with an interrogative pronoun has the same word order as that of a declarative sentence. Questions of this kind can be formed by substituting an interrogative pronoun for the word or phrase in the declarative sentence to be asked about. E.g.

他是 Gǔbō 。——他是誰？

她是大夫。——誰是大夫？

這是書。——這是什麼？

那是我的書。——那是誰的書？

他是 Zhōngguó 人。——他是哪國人？

2. Pronouns

Personal pronouns	Interrogative pronouns	Demonstrative pronouns
我　你　他　她 我們　你們　他們　她們	誰 什麼 哪	這　那

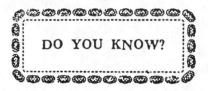
Beijing, Shanghai, the Changjiang (Yangtze) River,
the Huanghe (Yellow) River and the Great Wall

Beijing is the capital of the People's Republic of China, the country's chief political, economic and cultural centre.

Shanghai is China's biggest city, and her largest industrial centre as well.

The Changjiang (Yangtze) River, whose total length is 6,300 kilometres, is the longest river in China and one of the longest rivers in the world.

The Huanghe (Yellow) River is the second largest with a total length of 5,464 kilometres. The Huanghe valley was the cradle of the ancient Chinese civilization.

The Great Wall, which was built over 2,000 years ago, is one of the world's wonders in ancient architecture. Its total length is more than 2,500 kilometres, but quite a number of places are made up of several walls, the actual length comes to over 6,000 kilometres (more than 12,000 *li*). And for this reason it is also known as the "Great Wall of Ten Thousand *li*).

第 八 課

一、課 文

請 喝 茶

Gubo:　　Wáng Lǎoshī, nín hǎo!
Wáng 老師，您好！

Wang:　　Nǐ hǎo, qǐng jìn!
你好，請進！

Gubo:　　Zhè shì wǒ péngyou—Pàlánkǎ.
這是我朋友— Pàlánkǎ 。

Wang:　　Huānyíng, huānyíng. Qǐng hē chá.
歡迎，歡迎。請喝茶。

Palanka:　Xièxie.
謝謝。

Wang:　　Bú kèqi. Nǐ xī yān ma?
不客氣。你吸煙嗎？

Palanka:　Wǒ bù xī yān.
　　　　　我不吸煙。

二、生　詞

1.請	qǐng	please
2.喝	hē	to drink
3.茶	chá	tea
4.您	nín	polite form of "你"
5.進	jìn	to enter, to come in
6.歡迎	huānyíng	to welcome
7.謝謝	xièxie	to thank
8.客氣	kèqi	polite, courteous
9.吸煙	xī yān	to smoke

專　名

Wáng　　　　　a surname

補　充　詞

1. kāfēi　　　　coffee
2. píjiǔ　　　　beer
3. niúnǎi　　　milk

4. xiānsheng   Mr., sir, gentleman

5. tàitai   Mrs., madame

請 喝 茶

三、注釋 Notes

1. "Wáng 老師，您好！"

In Chinese, the surname precedes instead of following any form of address, e.g. "Wáng Dàifu", "Dīng Xiānsheng (Mr. Ding)".

"您" is the polite form of the pronoun for the second person singular "你". It is normally used to address one's elders and betters, as in "您好". For the sake of politeness or courtesy it is also used to address someone of one's own age, especially when meeting him or her for the first time.

2. "請進！"

"Come in, please."

"請…" is an expression of polite request.

3. "不客氣。"

"不客氣" is used in polite reply to expressions of thanks from others.

4. "你吸煙嗎？"

"Do you smoke?"

四、語音練習與會話練習
Pronunciation Drills and Conversation Practice

(一)

Initials	(j)	q	x
Finals	in	ian	uan

1. The four tones

qīng	qíng	qǐng	qìng	} qǐng jìn
jīn	jín	jǐn	jìn	
xiē	xié	xiě	xiè	— xièxie

xī   xí   xǐ   xì } xī yān
yān   yán   yǎn   yàn

kē   ké   kě   kè } kèqi
qī   qí   qǐ   qì

huān huán huǎn huàn } huānyíng
yīng yíng yǐng yìng

2. Combinations of tones

"–" + "–"   "–" + "/"   "–" + "ˇ"

   xī yān   Zhōngguó   qiānbǐ(pencil)

   kāfēi   huānyíng   tīngxiě (to have
                                        dictation)

"–" + "\"   "–" + "o*"

jīqì (machine)   tāmen

jīngjù (Beijing opera)   xiānsheng

3. Tone changes – half 3rd tone

   qǐng jìn

   qǐng hē chá

   qǐng xī yān

4. Read out the following disyllabic words:

   kàn jiàn (to see)   xiūxi (to rest)

   niánqīng (young)   qǐ chuáng (to get up)

   xǐhuan (to like)   shíxí (to practise)

   diànyǐng (film, movie)   duànliàn (to take exercise)

   yínháng (bank)   jīnnián (this year)

5. Try to pronounce the following polysyllables in quick succession:

   Wǒ niàn.   (I'll read it.)

   Nǐmen tīng.   (You'll listen, please.)

"o" in the "Combinations of Tones" of this lesson and the later lessons stands for the neutral tone.

Gēn wǒ niàn.   (Read it after me.)

Qǐng nǐ niàn.   (You please read it.)

Hěn hǎo.   (Very good.)

(一)

Entertaining a guest

(1) A: Wáng Lǎoshī, nín hǎo!

    B: Huānyíng, huānyíng.

       Qǐng jìn!

> Wáng Dàifu
>
> Qián Tàitai
>
> Jīn Xiānsheng

(2) A: Nín hē shénme?

    B: Wǒ hē kāfēi.

> chá   niúnǎi
>
> píjiǔ

(3) A: Jīn Xiānsheng, qǐng hē chá.

    B: Xièxie.

    A: Bú kèqi.

> kāfēi
>
> píjiǔ

(4) A: Nǐ xī yān ma?

    B: Xièxie, wǒ bù xī(yān).

> hē chá   hē píjiǔ
>
> hē niúnǎi

(5) A: Wáng Lǎoshī shì nǎ guó rén?

    B: Wáng Lǎoshī shì Zhōngguó rén.

> Wáng Dàifu
>
> Jīn Lǎoshī
>
> Jiāng Xiānsheng

五、語音 Phonetics

1. How to pronounce these initials

Initial q[tɕʻ]

The initial "q[tɕʻ]" is the correspondent aspirated to the unaspirated "j".

(73, 74)   — 56 —

Initial x[ɕ]

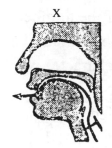

The initial "x[ɕ]" is produced by raising the front of the tongue to (but not touching) the hard palate leaving a narrow opening through which the air escapes causing audible friction. The vocal cords do not vibrate in producing this sound.

2. Rules of phonetic spelling

When forming syllables by themselves, "in" and "ing" are written as "yin" and "ying" respectively.

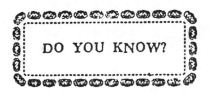

DO YOU KNOW?

The Complex and Simplified Forms of Chinese Characters

This textbook is available in two editions—one using the "complex" or "traditional" form of Chinese writing, the other using the "simplified" form created by the government of the People's Republic of China. While serious students of Chinese will eventually need to learn both forms, teachers have differed in their opinions about which writing form beginning students should be taught first. In recent years, the trend seems to be moving in the direction of teaching the complex forms first, as students seem to have an easier time picking up the simplified forms later.

As for China's long-term goals, the ultimate aim of the reform being carried out in the Chinese writing system is gradually to replace the ideograms with a phonetic writing system. Before this can be done, the characters need first of all to be simplified and the number of strokes of the characters reduced, so as to relieve much of the burden of both users and learners of Chinese. The simplification of Chinese characters is twofold: reduction of the number of the characters (mainly through the elimination of the complex variants) and reduction of the number of the strokes of which a complex character is composed (by the popularization of the simplified characters).

A few examples of the differences between the simplified forms and the complex forms are: "们（們）", "妈（媽）", "欢（歡）" and "进（進）".

Should you wish to learn both forms, this textbook is available in the simplified character form as well.

第 九 課

一、課 文

您 貴 姓

Palanka:　Qǐngwèn, nín shì Zhōngguó rén ma?
請問，您是 Zhōngguó 人嗎？

Ding Yun: Shì, wǒ shì Zhōngguó liúxuéshēng.
是，我是 Zhōngguó 留學生。

Palanka:　Nín guì xìng?
您貴姓？

Ding Yun: Wǒ xìng Dīng, Wǒ jiào Dīng Yún.
我姓 Dīng ，我叫 Dīng Yún 。

Palanka:　Wǒ jiào Pàlánkǎ, shì Wàiyǔ Xuéyuàn de xuésheng. Wǒ xuéxí Hànyǔ.
我叫 Pàlánkǎ ，是外語學院的學生。我學習漢語。

二、生 詞

1.貴姓　　　　　guì xìng　　　　What's your name? May I ask your name?

(79, 80)

2. 請問	qǐngwèn	May I ask. . .?
問	wèn	to ask
3. 留學生	liúxuéshēng	a student who studies abroad
4. 姓	xìng	(one's) surname is. . ., surname
5. 叫	jiào	to call, to be called
6. 外語	wàiyǔ	foreign language
7. 學院	xuéyuàn	college, institute
8. 學生	xuésheng	student
9. 學習	xuéxí	to study, to learn
學	xué	to study, to learn

專　名

| Dīng Yún | a personal name |

補　充　詞

1. xiǎojiě	miss
2. nǚshì	a polite form of address to a woman, lady, madam
3. tóngzhì	comrade
4. Cháoxiǎn	Korea
5. Yīngguó	Britain

(80, 81)

三、注釋 Notes

1. "請問"

    "May I ask. . .?" or "Excuse me, but. . . ."

    It is a polite form of inquiry, used to ask someone something.

2. "您貴姓？"

    "What's your surname?"

    It is a polite way of asking someone's surname. The person thus asked may give just his or her surname, i.e. "我姓…" or his or her name in full. i.e. "我叫…".

3. "我姓 Ding, 我叫 Ding Yun。"

    "My surname is Ding, and my name is Ding Yun."

四、語音練習與會話練習
Pronunciation Drills and Conversation Practice

(一)

```
Initials   (j      q      x)
Finals     iao
           uei(-ui)      uai          uen(-un)
           üe  üan  ün
```

1. The four tones

jiāo	jiáo	jiǎo	jiào
xīng	xíng	xǐng	xìng
wēn	wén	wěn	wèn — qǐngwèn
guī	guí	guǐ	guì — guì xìng
xuē	xué	xuě	xuě
shēng	shéng	shěng	shèng

> } xuésheng (for xuě / shěng pair)

| liū | liú | liŭ | liù | — liúxuéshēng |

wāi   wái   wăi   wài — wàiyŭ

yuān   yuán   yuăn   yuàn — xuéyuàn

xī   xí   xĭ   xī   — xuéxí

2. Combinations of tones

" ˇ " + " — "   " ˇ " + " ′ "   " ˇ " + " ˇ "

lăoshī   nă guó   nĭ hăo

Běijīng   qĭ chuáng   liăojiě (to understand)
                       (to get up)

" ˇ " + " ` "   " ˇ " + " o "

qĭngwèn   wŏmen

nŭshì   xiăojie

3. Read out the following dissyllabic words:

juéxīn (determination)   yuànyì (to be willing)

yúkuài (happy, pleasant)   huídá (to answer)

wèntí (question, problem) yīnyuè (music)

zhŭnbèi (to prepare)   jiàoshì (classroom)

kèwén (text)   Lŭ Xùn (Lu Xun)

4. Try to pronounce the following polysyllables in quick succession:

niàn kèwén (to read aloud the text)

kàn kèwén (to read the text)

wèn wèntí (to ask questions)

huídá wèntí (to answer questions)

Wŏ wèn.   (I'll ask a question.)

Nĭmen huídá.   (You answer it.)

Duì bu duì? (Is it right or wrong?)

Duì. (It is right.)

(一)

1. Asking about nationalities

   (1) A: Qǐngwèn, nín shì <u>Zhōngguó</u> rén ma?

       B: Shì, wǒ shì Zhōngguó rén.

   > Cháoxiǎn Mǎlǐ
   > Déguó

   (2) A: Qǐngwèn, nín shì <u>Rìběn</u> rén ma?

       B: Bù, wǒ shì Zhongguó rén.

   > Zhōngguó, Cháoxiǎn
   > Fǎguó,   Yīngguó
   > Yīngguó,   Měiguó

2. Asking about surnames and names

   (1) A: Qǐngwèn <u>dàifu</u>, nín guì xìng?

       B: Wǒ xìng _____ , jiào _____ :

       A: Wǒ jiào _____ .

   > xiǎojie   nǚshì
   > xiānsheng tóngzhì
   > tàitai

   (2) A: Qǐngwèn, nín shì <u>Wáng Xiānsheng</u> ma?

       B: Shì.

       A: Nín hǎo.

   > Dīng Xiǎojie   Wáng Nǚshì
   > Jīn Lǎoshī   Zhāng Tóngzhì

   (3) A: Tā xìng shénme?   A: Tā jiào shénme?

       B: Tā xìng_____ .   B: Tā jiào_____ .

— 63 —   (84, 85)

五、語音 Phonetics

1. How to pronounce the compound final

Compound final üe[yɛ]

The compound final "üe[yɛ]" is produced by articulating "ü" first, then promptly gliding to "ê". "ê" should be pronounced much louder and longer than "ü".

2. Rules of phonetic spelling

"uei" and "uen", when preceded by an initial, are written as "ui" and "un" respectively. When "ui" comes after an initial, the tone-graph is placed above "i".

When "ü" and the finals that begin with "ü" appear after "j". "q" or "x". "ü" is written as "u", with the two dots omitted, e.g. "xuexı".

您　貴　姓

第 十 課

一、課 文

她 住 多 少 號

Palanka:　Qǐngwèn, Dīng Yún zài ma?
請問，Dīng Yún 在嗎？

Zhongguo 　Tā bú zài, qǐng zuò.
xuesheng:　她不在，請坐。

Palanka:　Xièxie. Tā zài nǎr?
謝謝。她在哪兒？

Zhongguo 　Tā zài sùshè.
xuesheng:　她在宿舍。

Palanka:　Tā zhù duōshao hào?
她住多少號？

Zhongguo 　Sìcéng sìèrsān hào.
xuesheng:　四層四二三號。

　　　　　　　　(88, 89)

Palanka: Xièxie nǐ.

謝謝你。

*   *   *

líng   yī   èr   sān   sì   wǔ

〇   一   二   三   四   五

二、生　詞

1.在	zài	to be at (a place), in, at
2.坐	zuò	to sit, to take a seat
3.哪兒	nǎr	where
4.宿舍	sùshè	dormitory
5.住	zhù	to live
6.多少	duōshao	how many, how much, what
7.號	hào	number
8.四	sì	four
9.層	céng	(a measure word) storey, floor
10.二	èr	two
11.三	sān	three
12.〇	líng	zero
13.一	yī	one
14.五	wǔ	five

(89, 90)

補 充 詞

1. yīyuàn   hospital
2. cèsuǒ   toilet, latrine, lavatory, W.C.
3. zhèr   here
4. nàr   there

三、注釋 Notes

1. "Dīng Yún 在嗎？"
   "Is Ding Yun here?"

"在" here is a verb.

2. "她住多少號？"
   "What's her room number?"

3. "四層四二三號。"
   "No. 423, 4th floor."

By the Chinese reckoning, the different storeys of a building are numbered from the very ground level up.

四、語音練習與會話練習
Pronunciation Drills and Conversation Practice

(一)

Initials	z	c	s
Finals	-i[ʅ]		er

1. The four tones

zāi	(zái)	zǎi	zài	— zài ma
zuō	zuó	zuǒ	zuò	— qǐng zuò
cēng	céng	(cěng)	cèng	
sī	sí	sǐ	sì	— sì céng
sū	sú	(sǔ)	sù	— sù shè
sān	sán	sǎn	sàn	
(ēr)	ér	ěr	èr	
duō	duó	duǒ	duò	} duōshao
shāo	sháo	shǎo	shào	

2. Combinations of tones

    " ˊ " + " ─ "   " ˊ " + " ˊ "   " ˊ " + " ˇ "

    Cháng jiāng   xuéxí   Cháoxiǎn

    túshū (books)   Chángchéng   cáichǎn (property)

    " ˊ " + " ˋ "   " ˊ " + " o "

    xuéyuàn   péngyou

    búcuò (not bad)   érzi

3. Final "er" and retroflex final

    èr   érzi (son)

    nàr   ěrduo (ear)

    nǎr   nǚ'ér (daughter)

    zhèr   wánr (to play)

4. Read out the following dissyllabic words:

    zìjǐ (self)   cuòwu (mistake, error)

    qúnzi (skirt)   cóngcǐ (from now on)

    xǐzǎo (to take a bath)   cānguān (to visit)

    qīzi (wife)   Hànzì (Chinese character)

    shēngcí (new word)   Sūlián (the Soviet Union)

5. Try to pronounce the following polysyllables in quick succession:

    shuō Hànyǔ (to speak Chinese)

    niàn shēngcí (to read aloud new words)

    xiě Hànzì (to write Chinese characters)

    tīng lùyīn (to listen to recordings)

    zuò liànxí (to do exercises)

    fānyi jùzi (to translate sentences)

    jiǎng yǔfǎ (to explain grammar)

    Dǒng bu dǒng? (Do you understand?)

    Dǒng. (Yes, I do.)

1. Asking for someone

    (1) A: Dīng Yún zài ma?

         B: Zài. Qǐng jìn.

> Wáng Nǚshì
>
> Dīng Xiǎojie
>
> Jīn Dàifu

    (2) A: Qǐng wèn, Dīng Yún zài ma?

         B: Tā bú zài.

         A: Tā zài nǎr?

         B: Tā zài sùshè.

> yīyuàn
>
> xuéyuàn
>
> nàr

2. Asking about addresses

    (1) A: Nǐ zhù nǎr?

         B: Wǒ zhù zhèr.

         A: Nǐ zhù duōshao hào?

         B: Wǒ zhù sìcéng sìsān'èr hào.

> 2 — 201
>
> èr—èrlíngyī
>
> 4 — 425
>
> sì—sìèrwǔ

    (2) A: Nín guì xìng?

         B: Wǒ xìng Dīng, jiào Dīng Yún.

A: Nín zhù nǎr?

B: Wǒ zhù yī,èrwǔ hào.

422
sìèrèr
124
yīèrsì

3. Asking the way

A: Qǐngwèn, Wàiyǔ Xuéyuàn zài nǎr?

B: Zài nàr.

sùshè
yīyuàn
cèsuǒ

五、語音 Phonetics

1. How to pronounce these initials and finals

Initial z[ts]

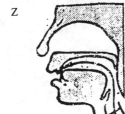

z

The initial "z[ts]" is produced by first pressing the tip of the tongue against the back of the upper teeth, then lowering it to let the air squeeze out through the narrow opening thus made. It is unaspirated. The vocal cords do not vibrate when producing this sound.

Initial c[tsʻ]

c

The initial "c[tsʻ]" is an aspirated consonant corresponding to the unaspirated "z".

– 71 –

(94, 95)

Initial s[s]

s

The initial "s[s]" is produced by pressing the tip of the tongue to (but not against) the back of the upper teeth, forming a narrow opening through which the air escapes causing audible friction. The vocal cords do not vibrate when producing it.

Simple final -i[ʅ]

The letter "-i" is sometimes used to stand for the blade-alveolar vowel [ʅ] when it occurs after such initials as "z", "c" and "s". (Care must be taken, however, not to pronounce "-i" as [i].) The sound "-i[ʅ]" comes only after "z", "c" and "s". It never comes after any other initials, nor does it occur as an independent final.

Simple final er[ər]

The simple final "er[ər]" is produced in the same way as "e", but with the tongue curled and raised towards the hard palate.

2. Retroflex final

The final "er" is sometimes attached to another final to form a retroflex final and when thus used, it is no longer an independent syllable. A retroflex final is represented by the letter "r" added to the final. In actual writing, "兒" is added to the character is question, as in "wánr (玩兒)".

3. Rules of phonetic spelling

When a syllable beginning with "a", "o" or "e" follows another syllable in such an ambiguous way that division of the two syllables could be confused, it is essential to put a dividing mark " ' " in between, e.g. "nǚ'er".

六、語法 Grammar

Sentences with a verbal predicate

A sentence with a verbal predicate is one in which the main element of the predicate is a verb. One way to make such a sentence negative is to put the adverb "不" before the predicative verb, indicating "One does not, will not do something or is not willing to do something".

Nouns or pronouns	Adverb	Verbs	Particle
Dīng Yún （她） 她	 不	在 在。 在。	嗎？

The object, if the verb takes one, usually comes after the verb.

Nouns or pronouns	Adverb	Verbs	Nouns or pronouns	Particle
你 我 我 我	 不	吸 吸 學習 叫	煙 煙。 漢語。 Pàlánkǎ。	嗎？

(97, 98)

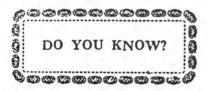
China's Minority Nationalities and Their Languages

China is a country of many nationalities, with 94% of her population belonging to the Han nationality. Apart from the Hans, there are more than 50 other nationalities such as the Monggols (Mongolians), the Huis, the Zangs (Tibetans), the Uygurs (Uighurs), the Miaos, the Yis, the Zhuangs, the Buyis, the Koreans, the Mans (Manchus) and the Gaoshans.

All of China's minority nationalities have languages of their own (some have their own written languages) with the exception only of the Hui, Man and She nationalities who use Chinese or the language of the Hans. The Chinese Constitution stipulates that all the nationalities of China have the freedom to use and further develop their spoken and written languages. In order to rapidly develop the culture and education of the minority nationalities, the government has helped the Zhuang, Miao, Jingpo and other minority nationalities to devise their own written languages based on the Latin alphabet or to improve their existing writing system.

第十一課

一、課　文

謝　謝　你

Ding Yun: Huán nǐ huàbào, xièxie.
還你畫報，謝謝。

Palanka: Bú xiè. Nà shì Hànyǔ cídiǎn ma?
不謝。那是漢語詞典嗎？

Ding Yun: (Nà) shì Hànyǔ cídiǎn.
（那）是漢語詞典。

Palanka: Nǐ xiànzài yòng ma?
你現在用嗎？

Ding Yun: Bú yòng. Nǐ yòng ma?
不用。你用嗎？

Palanka: Wǒ yòng yíxiàr.
我用一下兒。

(102, 103)

Ding Yun: Hǎo.

好。

Palanka: Xièxie nǐ.

謝謝你。

Ding Yun: Bú kèqi.

不客氣。

Palanka: Zàijiàn!

再見！

Ding Yun: Zàijiàn!

再見！

*   *   *

liù   qī   bā   jiǔ   shí

六   七   八   九   十

二、生 詞

1. 還	huán	to return
2. 畫報	huàbào	pictorial
3. 詞典	cídiǎn	dictionary
4. 現在	xiànzài	now, nowadays
5. 用	yòng	to use, to make use of
6. 一下兒	yíxiàr	a little while

(103, 104)

7.再見	zàijiàn	to say good-bye, to bid farewell to
8.六	liù	six
9.七	qī	seven
10.八	bā	eight
11.九	jiǔ	nine
12.十	shí	ten

補 充 詞

1. zázhì		magazine
2. diànhuà		telephone, telephone call
3. běnzi		note-book, exercise-book
4. yǔsǎn		umbrella

三、注釋 Notes

1. "還你畫報。"
   "Here is the pictorial (I borrowed from you)."
2. "我用一下兒。"
   "May I use it for a while?"
" 一下兒 " here means "a little while" or "a short time".

四、語音練習與會話練習
Pronunciation Drills and Conversation Practice

㈠

Initials	(z	c	s)
Finals	u*a*	i*a*	ï*ong*

1. The four tones

   zāi   (zái)   zǎi   zài — zàijiàn
   cī   cí   cǐ   cì   — cídiǎn
   huā   huá   (huǎ) huà — huàbào
   xiā   xiá   (xiǎ) xià — yíxiàr
   yōng   yóng   yǒng   yòng

2. Combinations of tones

   " ˋ " + " ˉ "   " ˋ " + " ˊ "   " ˋ " + " ˇ "
   zuòjiā (writer)   dìtú   Hànyǔ
   miànbāo (bread)   liànxí (exercise)   wàiyǔ
   " ˋ " + " ˋ "   " ˋ " + " ˳ "
       huàbào   xièxie
       zàijiàn   tàitai

3. Retroflex final

huār (flower)   yìdiǎnr (a little, a bit)
yíxiàr   yíhuìr (in a moment)

4. Read out the following dissyllabic words:

cānjiā (to take part in)   bǐsài (competition, match)
zhuōzi (table)   cèyàn (test, quiz)
cāochǎng (sports-field)   Yà Zhōu (Asia)
cíqì (porcelain)   huá bīng (to skate, skating)
yǒngyuǎn (forever)   xióngmāo (panda)

5. Try to pronounce the following polysyllables in quick succession:

Hànyǔ cídiǎn (Chinese dictionary)
Hànyǔ lǎoshī (a teacher of Chinese)
wàiyǔ xuéyuàn (institute of foreign languages)
xuésheng sùshè (students' dormitory)
Zhōngguó dìtú (a Chinese map)
Zhōngguó liúxuéshēng (a Chinese student who studies abroad)

(二)

1. Expressing one's thanks to someone

(1)

A: _____ :

B: _____ :

(2) A: Qǐng zuò:
    B: Xièxie.
    A: Bú kèqi.

| jìn |
| hē chá |
| hē kāfēi |

(3) A: Huánnǐ dìtú.
         Xièxie nǐ.
      B: Bú xiè.

shū	cídiǎn
bǐ	běnzi
zázhì	yǔsǎn

2. Saying good-bye to someone:

A: _____ :
B: _____ :

3. Asking about telephone numbers
       A: Qǐngwèn, nǐ de diànhuà
          hào shì duōshao?
       B: èrliùbāqīwǔjiǔ.

728064
qīērbālíngliùsì
870492
bāqīlíngsìjiǔèr

五、語音 Phonetics

Compound finals

The second elements in such compound finals as "ia[ia]", "ie", "üa [ua]", "uo" and "üe" are pronounced louder than the first ones, with their volume becoming greater gradually but not abruptly. The second elements are full vowels and should be given their full value in pronunciation.

The first elements in such compound finals as "ai", "ei", "ao" and "ou" are pronounced louder than the second ones, with their volume becoming smaller gradually but not abruptly. The second elements indicate the directions towards which the vowels move rather than the limits.

In the compound finals "iao", "iou", "uai" and "uei" the medial elements are pronounced loudest.

(107, 108)

Care must be taken that, in the pronunciation of the compound finals above mentioned, the movement from one vowel to another is one of gliding but not abrupt jumping.

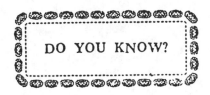

DO YOU KNOW?

Chinese Dictionaries

The most popular current Chinese dictionaries are " 新華字典 " dealing mainly with individual characters, which contains about 8,000 entries, and " 現代漢語詞典 ", a medium-sized dictionary containing more than 56,000 entries. Among the large-sized dictionaries are " 辭海 " and " 辭源 ".

第十二課

一、課 文

她們是很好的朋友

Pàlánkǎ shì Gǔbō de nǚ péngyou. Xiànzài tāmen dōu xuéxí Hànyǔ. Tāmen lǎoshī
Pàlánkǎ 是 Gǔbō 的女朋友。現在他們都學習漢語。他們老師

xìng Wáng, shì Zhōngguó rén. Wáng Xiānsheng shì tāmen de lǎoshī, yě shì tāmen de
姓 Wáng ，是 Zhōngguó 人。Wáng 先生是他們的老師，也是他們的

péngyou.
朋友。

Pàlánkǎ rènshi Zhōngguó liúxuéshēng Dīng Yún. Dīng Yún xuéxí Yīngyǔ, yě xuéxí
Pàlánkǎ 認識 Zhōngguó 留學生 Dīng Yún。Dīng Yún 學習英語，也學

Fǎyǔ. Pàlánkǎ cháng qù xuésheng sùshè kàn tā. Tāmen shì hěn hǎo de péngyou.
習法語。Pàlánkǎ 常去學生宿舍看她。她們是很好的朋友。

二、生 詞

1.女　　　　　nǚ　　　　　female

2.先生	xiānsheng	Mr., sir, gentleman
3.認識	rènshi	to know, to be familiar with, to recognize
4.英語	Yīngyǔ	English
5.法語	Fǎyǔ	French
6.常	cháng	often
7.去	qù	to go
8.她們	tāmen	they, them

(112, 113)

三、注釋 Notes

1. "Pàlánkǎ 常去學生宿舍看她。"
   "Palanka often goes to the students' dormitory to see her."
2. "她們是很好的朋友。"
   "They are good friends."
3. "Dīng Yún 學習英語，也學習法語。"

The idea of "the language of a certain nation" is expressed in Chinese by adding the word "語, yǔ" or "文, wén" (both here meaning "language") to the short form of the name of the nation (the word "國", if there is one in the Chinese, should be dropped), as in "英語", "法語".

四、語音復習 Phonetics Review

1. A brief summary of the finals and initials

韵母 Finals	單韵母 Simple finals
	a[a]　　o[o]　　e[ɤ]　　ê[ɛ]　　i[i]　　u[u]　　ü[y]
	-i[ɿ][ʅ]　　　　er[ər]
	復韵母 Compound finals
	ai[ai]　　ei[ei]　　ao[au]　　ou[əu]
	ia[ia]　　ie[iɛ]　　iao[iau]　　iou(-iu)[iəu]
	ua[ua]　　uo[uo]　　uai[uai]　　uei(-ui)[uei]
	üe[yɛ]
	鼻韵母 Nasal finals
	an[an]　　en[ən]　　　　ang[aŋ]　eng[əŋ]　ong[uŋ]
	ian[iɛn]　in[in]　　　　iang[iaŋ]　ing[iŋ]　iong[iuŋ]
	uan[uan]　uen(-un)[uən]　uang[uaŋ]　　　ueng*[uəŋ]
	üan[yan]　ün[yn]

Initials 聲母	唇音 Labials	b[p]	p[p']	m[m]	f[f]
	舌尖音 Alveolars	d[t]	t[t']	n[n]	l[1]
	舌尖前音 Blade-alveolars	z[ts]	c[ts']	s[s]	
	舌尖後音 Blade-palatals	zh[tʂ]	ch[tʂ']	sh[ʂ]	
		r[ʐ]			
	舌面音 Alveolars	j[tɕ]	q[tɕ']	x[ɕ]	
	舌根音 Velars	g[k]	k[k]	h[x]	

(1) Vowels predominate in Chinese syllables. A syllable can consist of two consonants at most, which can never follow each other but must always be separated by a vowel.

(2) Modern Chinese has altogether 21 initials only a few of which are voiced, i.e. "r, m, n" and "l", and the rest are all voiceless.

(3) In the 21 initials there are 6 paris of corresponding initials (12 in all) in which 6 are aspirated and the other are unaspirated. Since in Chinese aspiration or the lack of it is capable of differenciating meaning, care must be taken to pronounce the sounds correctly and not to confuse the aspirated sounds with the unaspirated ones or vice versa.

(4) Every syllable in Chinese has its specific tone. Change of tone involves change of meaning. So, in learning a new word, we should bear in mind what tone it has as well as what change in tone there should be under a given condition.

2. A brief summary of the rules of phonetic spelling

   i — y(yi):

      i — yi   ian — yan
      ia — ya   in   — yin
      ie — ye   iang — yang

---

*The nasal final "ueng", which has not appeared in any of the preceding 11 lessons, never occurs after an initial but always forms a syllable by itself.

```
iao  –  yao          ing   –  ying
iou  –  you          iong  –  yong
```
u – w(wu):
```
u    –  wu           uan   –  wan
ua   –  wa           uen   –  wen
uo   –  wo           uang  –  wang
uai  –  wai          ueng  –  weng
uei  –  wei
```
ü – yu:
```
ü    –  yu           üan   –  yuan
üe   –  yue          ün    –  yun
```

五、語音練習與會話練習
Pronunciation Drills and Conversation Practice

㈠

1. Sound discrimination
   (1) The aspirated and unaspirated sounds
   ```
   b – p        z – c
   d – t        zh – ch
   g – k        j – q
   ```
   ```
            *        *        *
   ```
   b – biǎoyáng (to praise)   d – dàifu
   p – piāoyáng (to flutter)   t – tàidu (attitude)
   zh – zhīdao (to know)   j – dǎ jiǔ (to buy some wine)
   ch – chídào (to be late)   q – dǎ qiú (to play basketball)
   g – gānjìng (clean, neat)
   k – kàn qīng (to see clearly)
   z – xǐzǎo (to take a bath)
   c – chú cǎo (to weed, weeding)

(2) Alveolar-finals and velar-finals

an — dànshì (but, however)

ang — dāngshí (at that time)

ian — liánxì (contact)

iang — liángkuai (nice and cool)

uan — zhuānjiā (expert)

uang — zhuāngjia (crops)

en — pénzi (basin)

eng — péngyou (friend)

in — rénmín (people)

ing — rénmíng (a personal name)

2. Half 3rd tone

Nǐ hē chá ma?   Nǐ kàn shénme?

Nǐ xī yān ma?   Nǐ xìng shénme?

Nǐ yòng cídiǎn ma?   Nǐ jiào shénme?

Wǒ xuéxi Hànyǔ.

Wǒ rènshı tā.

Wǒ zhù sùshè.

3. Trisyllabic words

túshūguǎn (library)   zhàoxiàngjī (camera)

yuèlǎnshì (reading-room)   zìxíngchē (bicycle)

liúxuéshēng   huǒchēzhàn (railway stution)

shōuyīnjī (radio)   bàngōngshì (office)

Try to pronounce the following polysyllables in quick succession:

fùxí kèwén (to review the text)

yùxí shēngcí (to preview new words)

zhùyì fāyīn (to pay attention to pronunciation)

zhùyì shēngdiào (to pay attention to tones)

zài niàn yíbiàn (Read it again.)

zài xiě yíbiàn (Write it once more.)

4. Read out the following poem:

Jìng Yè Sī

Lǐ Bái

Chuáng qián míng yuè guāng,
Yí shì dì shàng shuāng.
Jǔ tóu wàng míng yuè,
Dī tóu sī gùxiāng.

Homesickness On a Quiet Night
by Li Bai

On the ground before my bed
Is spread the bright moonlight,
But I take it for frost
When I wake up at the first sight.
Then I look up at the bright full moon in the sky,
Suddenly homesickness strikes me as I bow my head
With a deep sigh.

(一)

1. Read out the following dialogues:
   (1) A: Shéi? Qǐng jìn!
       B: Nǐ hǎo!
       A: Nǐ hǎo. Qǐng zuò.
       B: Nǐ máng ma?
       A: Bù máng. Qǐng hē chá.
       B: Xièxie.
   (2) A: Nín shì Rìběn rén ma?
       B: Bú shì.
       A: Nín shì nǎ guó rén?

B: Wǒ shì Zhōngguó rén.

A: Nín guì xìng?

B: Wǒ xìng Wáng. Nín ne?

A: Wǒ shì Yīngguó rén. Wǒ xìng Gélín.

(3) A: Nín hǎo, tàitai!

B: Nín hǎo!

A: Qǐngwèn, Lǐ Xiānsheng zài ma?

B: Zài. Qǐng jìn.

C: À, shì nǐ. Qǐng zuò, qǐng zuò.

B: Nín hē kāfēi ma?

A: Xièxie.

2. Say as much as you can about each of the following pictures:

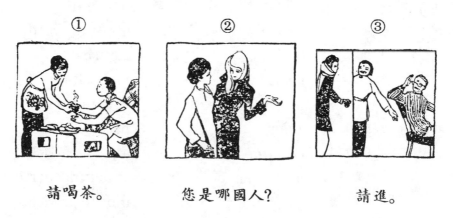

① 請喝茶。　　　② 您是哪國人？　　　③ 請進。

詞類簡稱表

Abbreviations

1. （名） 名詞   míngcí   noun
   （專名）專有名詞   zhuānyǒu
       míngcí   proper name
2. （代） 代詞   dàicí   pronoun
3. （動） 動詞   dòngcí   verb
4. （能動）能願動詞   néngyuàn dòngcí   optative verb
5. （形） 形容詞   xíngróngcí   adjective
6. （數） 數詞   shùcí   numeral
7. （量） 量詞   liàngcí   measure word
8. （副） 副詞   fùcí   adverb
9. （介） 介詞   jiècí   preposition
10. （連） 連詞   liáncí   conjunction
11. （助） 助詞   zhùcí   particle
    動態助詞   dòngtài zhùcí   aspect particle
    結構助詞   jiégòu zhùcí   structural particle
    語氣助詞   yǔqì zhùcí   modal particle
12. （嘆） 嘆詞   tàncí   interjection
13. （象聲）象聲詞   xiàngshēngcí   onomatopoeia
    （頭） 詞頭   cítóu   prefix
    （尾） 詞尾   cíwěi   suffix

Table of the Combinations of the Initials and Finals in Common Speech

声母＼韵母	a	o	e	ê	-i	er	ai	ei	ao	ou	an	en	ang	eng	ong	i	ia	iao	ie	iu
	a	o	e	ê		er	ai	ei	ao	ou	an	en	ang	eng		yi	ya	yao	ye	you
b	ba	bo					bai	bei	bao		ban	ben	bang	beng		bi		biao	bie	
p	pa	po					pai	pei	pao	pou	pan	pen	pang	peng		pi		piao	pie	
m	ma	mo	me				mai	mei	mao	mou	man	men	mang	meng		mi		miao	mie	miu
f	fa	fo						fei		fou	fan	fen	fang	feng						
d	da		de				dai	dei	dao	dou	dan	den	dang	deng	dong	di		diao	die	diu
t	ta		te				tai		tao	tou	tan		tang	teng	tong	ti		tiao	tie	
n	na		ne				nai	nei	nao	nou	nan	nen	nang	neng	nong	ni		niao	nie	niu
l	la		le				lai	lei	lao	lou	lan		lang	leng	long	li	lia	liao	lie	liu
z	za		ze		zi		zai	zei	zao	zou	zan	zen	zang	zeng	zong					
c	ca		ce		ci		cai		cao	cou	can	cen	cang	ceng	cong					
s	sa		se		si		sai		sao	sou	san	sen	sang	seng	song					
zh	zha		zhe		zhi		zhai	zhei	zhao	zhou	zhan	zhen	zhang	zheng	zhong					
ch	cha		che		chi		chai		chao	chou	chan	chen	chang	cheng	chong					
sh	sha		she		shi		shai	shei	shao	shou	shan	shen	shang	sheng						
r			re		ri				rao	rou	ran	ren	rang	reng	rong					
j																ji	jia	jiao	jie	jiu
q																qi	qia	qiao	qie	qiu
x																xi	xia	xiao	xie	xiu
g	ga		ge				gai	gei	gao	gou	gan	gen	gang	geng	gong					
k	ka		ke				kai	kei	kao	kou	kan	ken	kang	keng	kong					
h	ha		he				hai	hei	hao	hou	han	hen	hang	heng	hong					

ian	in	iang	ing	iong	u	ua	uo	uai	ui	uan	un	uang	ueng	ü	üe	üan	ün
yan	yin	yang	ying	yong	wu	wa	wo	wai	wei	wan	wen	wang	weng	yu	yue	yuan	yun
bian	bin		bing		bu												
pian	pin		ping		pu												
mian	min		ming		mu												
					fu												
dian			ding		du		duo		dui	duan	dun						
tian			ting		tu		tuo		tui	tuan	tun						
nian	nin	niang	ning		nu		nuo			nuan				nü	nüe		
lian	lia	liang	ling		lu		luo			luan	lun			lü	lüe		
					zu		zuo		zui	zuan	zun						
					cu		cuo		cui	cuan	cun						
					su		suo		sui	suan	sun						
					zhu	zhua	zhuo	zhuai	zhui	zhuan	zhun	zhuang					
					chu	chua	chuo	chuai	chui	chuan	chun	chuang					
					shu	shua	shuo	shuai	shui	shuan	shun	shuang					
					ru	rua	ruo		rui	ruan	run						
jian	jin	jiang	jing	jiong										ju	jue	juan	jun
qian	qin	qiang	qing	qiong										qu	que	quan	qun
xian	xin	xiang	xing	xiong										xu	xue	xuan	xun
					gu	gua	guo	guai	gui	guan	gun	guang					
					ku	kua	kuo	kuai	kui	kuan	kun	kuang					
					hu	hua	huo	huai	hui	huan	hun	huang					

第 十 三 課

一、課 文

你 認 識 不 認 識 她

古　波：你看，她是不是中國人？
Gubo:　Nǐ kàn, tā shì bu shì Zhōngguó rén?

帕蘭卡：是，她是中國人。
Palanka: shì, tā shì Zhōngguó rén.

古　波：你認識不認識她？
Gubo:　Nǐ rènshi bu rènshi tā?

帕蘭卡：我認識她。
Palanka: Wǒ rènshi tā.

古　波：她叫什麼名字？
Gubo:　Tā jiào shénme míngzi?

帕蘭卡：她叫丁雲。
Palanka: Tā jiào Dīng Yún.

　　　　　　　　　(123, 124)

喂，丁雲，你去哪兒？

Wèi, Dīng Yún, nǐ qù nǎr?

丁　雲：啊！是你，帕蘭卡。我去商店買筆。

Ding Yun:　À! shì nǐ, Palánkǎ. Wǒ qù shāngdiàn mǎi bǐ.

帕蘭卡：我們也去商店買紙。來，我介紹一下兒。這是我的中

Palanka:　Wǒmen yě qù shāngdiàn mǎi zhǐ. Lái, wǒ jièshào yíxiàr. Zhè shì wǒ de Zhōngguó

國朋友，丁雲。他是我的男朋友——

péngyǒu, Dīng Yún. Tā shì wǒ de nán péngyou--

古　波：我叫古波。你好！

Gubo:　Wǒ jiào Gǔbō. Nǐ hǎo!

丁　雲：你好！你也學習漢語嗎？

Ding Yun:　Nǐ hǎo! Nǐ yě xuéxí Hànyǔ ma?

古　波：對了，我和帕蘭卡都學漢語。

Gubo:　Dùi le, wǒ hé Palánkǎ dōu xué Hànyǔ.

帕蘭卡：他常說漢語。

Palanka:　Tā cháng shuō Hànyǔ.

二、生　詞

1.名字	míngzi	name
2.喂	wèi	an interjection, hello
3.啊	à	an interjection, oh

4.商店	shāngdiàn	shop
5.買	mǎi	to buy
6.筆	bǐ	pen
7.紙	zhǐ	paper
8.來	lái	to come
9.介紹	jièshào	to introduce
10.男	nán	male
11.對	duì	right, correct
12.了	le	a modal particle
13.和	hé	and, with
14.説	shuō	to speak, to say

專　　名

1.古波	Gǔbō	a personal name
2.中國	Zhōngguó	China
3.帕蘭卡	Pàlánkǎ	a personal name
4.丁雲	Dīng Yún	a personal name

補　充　詞

1.英國	Yīngguó	Britain
2.法國	Fǎguó	France

　　　　　　　(125, 126)

3.本子	běnzi	note-book, exercise-book
4.郵局	yóujú	post office
5.郵票	yóupiào	stamp
6.教授	jiàoshòu	professor

三、閱讀短文

帕蘭卡問古波："你認識丁雲嗎？"古波說，不認識。帕蘭卡說："你看，那是丁雲。來，我介紹一下兒。"

"喂，丁雲，你來一下兒。"帕蘭卡說，"這是古波，這是丁雲——我的中國朋友。"

古波說漢語："你好！"

丁雲問他："你也學習漢語嗎？"

"我和帕蘭卡都學習漢語。我們的漢語老師姓Wáng，你認識嗎？"

"認識，"丁雲說，"Wáng 老師常去宿舍看我們。"

"你學習什麼？"古波問她。

"我現在學習英語和法語。"

帕蘭卡問丁雲："你現在忙不忙？"

"我很忙。你爸爸、媽媽好嗎？"

"謝謝你，他們都很好。"帕蘭卡說。

四、注釋 Notes

1. "喂，丁雲，你去哪兒？"

"喂" is an interjection used to express informal greeting, equivalent to "hello" or "hey".

2. "啊，是你，帕蘭卡。"

"啊" is also an interjection. Here it is pronounced in the 4th tone, expressing unexpectedness or sudden realization.

3. "來，我介紹一下兒。"

"我介紹一下兒" is a common expression used while introducing people to each other. "一下兒" here softens the tone, making it sound informal.

4. "對了，我和帕蘭卡都學習漢語。"

In Chinese, the conjunction "和" is used to connect nouns, pronouns or nominal constructions only. No "和" is needed between two clauses and it is wrong to say "我買書，和他買筆". Nor is "和" often used to join verbs or verbal constructions.

五、替換與擴展 Substitution and Extension

(一)

1. 他是不是中國人？
   他是中國人。

| 大夫 | 英國*人 |
| 學生 | 法國*人 |

Words marked with the asterisk " * " are supplementary words.

2. 你認識不認識他?
   我不認識他。

他們	謝老師
丁雲	我朋友

3. 你說不說漢語?
   我說漢語。

英語	法語
外語	

4. 你買不買書?
   我不買書，我買地圖。

詞典,	書
畫報,	地圖
筆,	本子

5. 你去哪兒?
   我去商店買筆。

宿舍,	喝茶
學院,	還書
郵局,	買郵票
商店,	買紙

6. 你也學習漢語嗎?

我也學習漢語。

你們都學習漢語嗎?

對了，我們都學習漢語。

去，	中國
是，	學生
用，	詞典

(二)

1. Introducing people to each other

    A：你們認識嗎? 我介紹一下兒。

    　　這是丁教授˙。

    　　這是我的女朋友謝英。

    B：您好。

    C：您好。

2. Meeting each other

    A：請問，您叫什麼名字?

    B：我叫謝英。

    A：您是哪國人?

    B：我是中國人。

    A：您說英語嗎?

    B：我說英語。

3. Running into each other

    A：喂，謝英!

    B：啊，是你，丁朋! 你好。

    A：你好。你去哪兒?

— 99 —

(129, 130, 131)

B：我去商店買本子·，你去不去?

A：我也去。

*　　*　　*

名片 Mingpian, card

```
┌─────────────────────────────┐
│      北京語言學院敎授          │
│                             │
│      王　書　文              │
│                             │
│   北京語言學院 5 樓 3 號        │
│           電話　277531       │
└─────────────────────────────┘
```

六、語法 Grammar

1. Affirmative-negative questions

An affirmative-negative question is another form of question which is made by juxtaposing the affirmative and negative forms of the main element of the predicate (the predicative verb or adjective). Such a question has the same function as a general question with the interrogative particle " 嗎".

Nouns or pronouns	Affirmative forms of the predicative verb or adjective	Negative forms of the predicative verb or adjective	Nouns or pronouns
他 大夫 你 你哥哥	是 來 喝 認識	不是 不來? 不喝 不認識	學生? 茶? 她?

老師	忙	不忙?	
你的筆	好	不好?	

2. Sentences with verbal constructions in series

A sentence with verbal constructions in series is a sentence in which the predicate consists of more than one verb (or verbal construction) sharing the same subject. In a sentence of this kind, the verbs or verbal constructions follow a definite and unalterable order and admit no pause between them in actual speech.

Sentences of this type fall into several kinds. The kind covered in this lesson includes sentences having in their predicate two verbs the second of which denotes the purpose of the action expressed by the first. E.g.

Nouns or pronouns	Verbs (1)	Nouns	Verbs (2)	Nouns	Particles
你	去	外語學院	看	朋友	嗎?
我	去	學生宿舍	看	朋友。	
他	來	學院	問	老師。	
你	去		還	書	嗎?
我朋友	來		幫助	我。	

3. Position of the adverbs "也" and "都"

The adverbs "也" and "都" usually follow the subject but precede the predicative verb or adjective. Used simultaneously in a sentence to qualify the predicate, "也" must precede "都".

(133, 134, 135)

Nouns or pronouns	Adverbs	Verbs, verbal constructions or adjectives
我	也很	好。
我們	都很	好。
他	也不	是學生。
他們	都不	是學生。
我們	不都	是學生。
他	也	說漢語。
她們	也都	說漢語。

Note that, in a sentence, what "都" sums up usually refers to all the persons or things that go before it rather than what comes after it. Thus, we can only say "我們都認識他" but not "我都認識他們".

七、練習 Exercises

1. Read out the following phrases:

   (1) 是不是　喝不喝　還不還

   　　在不在　來不來　看不看

   　　問不問　用不用　坐不坐

   　　買不買　去不去　說不說

   　　學習不學習　認識不認識

介紹不介紹　　歡迎不歡迎

(2)　中國人　　　男人　　　女人

中國朋友　男朋友　女朋友

中國學生　男學生　女學生

中國老師　男老師　女老師

中國大夫　男大夫　女大夫

2. Make a general question with the interrogative particle " 嗎 " and an affirmative-negative question using each of the following verbs:

Example　　看　書

›他看書嗎?

他看不看書?

(1)　在

(2)　來

(3)　是　謝老師

(4)　喝　茶

(5)　用　車

(6)　在　宿舍

(7)　學習　漢語

(8)　說　英語

(9)　買　紙

3. Put in an appropriate phrase from the list below in each of the following sentences:

學習漢語　買筆

還書　　　看朋友

(1) 我去商店＿＿＿＿＿＿。

(2) 她去學生宿舍＿＿＿＿＿＿。

(3) 丁雲來學院＿＿＿＿＿＿。

(4) 他們去中國＿＿＿＿＿＿。

4. Rewrite the following sentences using "都":

Example　　帕蘭卡認識丁雲，古波也認識丁雲。

　　　　　→帕蘭卡和古波都認識丁雲。

(1) 他學習漢語，她也學習漢語。

(2) 我爸爸是大夫，我媽媽也是大夫。

(3) 他說英語，他朋友也說英語。

(4) 謝老師是中國人，丁雲也是中國人。

(5) 我去商店，我哥哥也去商店。

(6) 他不吸煙，他的女朋友也不吸煙。

(7) 丁雲不在宿舍，她朋友也不在宿舍。

(8) 我去外語學院看朋友，古波也去外語學院看朋友。

八、語音語調 Pronunciation and Intonation

1. Word stress (1)

Putonghua or the common speech of modern Chinese distinguishes roughly three degrees of strees of polysyllabic words: main (or strong) stress, medium stress and weak stress, which can be distinctly differentiated in the pronunciation of a word of many syllables. Words of two, three or four syllables have a distinct strong stress on one of the syllables (marked with the sign " · " in this book). In most dissyllabic words, the strong stress falls on the second syllable, and the first syllable is usually pronounced with a medium stress. E.g.

漢語　英語　詞典　地圖　畫報

學習　老師　丁雲　古波

再見　歡迎　商店　學院

A small number of dissyllabic words have the main stress falling on the first syllable, and the second syllable is usually pronounced with a weak stress even though it is normally not the neutral tone (with a tone-graph over it). E.g.

朋友　認識　名字　先生　學生

大夫　我們　什麼　介紹(動)學習 (動)

2. Exercises

(1) Read out the following phrases, paying attention to the changes of tone of " 不 ":

不說　不吸煙　不喝茶　不歡迎

不來　不還　不學習

(139, 140)

不買　不請

不去　不坐　不住　不看　不問

不用　不介紹　不認識

(2) Read out the following words containing the sounds zh, ch, sh, or r, paying attention to their pronunciation and word stress:

中國　日本　書店　宿舍　商店

介紹　認識　長城　長江　學生

(3) Read out the proverb:

shú　néng　shēng　qiǎo　(Practice makes perfect.)

熟　　能　　生　　巧

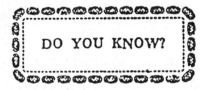

DO YOU KNOW?

Personal Names in China

The name of a Chinese (of the Han nationality or of some of China's minority nationalities) is made up of two elements, the surname and the given name, with the former always preceding the latter. Surnames or family names are usually monosyllabic characters, such as Ding, Wang, Li and Jin. Only a few Chinese surnames, such as Ouyang and Sima are dissyllabic. Given names consist sometimes of two characters, such as Shuwen, and sometimes of only one, such as Yun. In present-day China, women retain their own surnames after marriage. Traditionally children have the same surname as their father though there are occasional cases of children using their mother's surname.

(140, 143)

第 十 四 課

一、課 文

他 作 什 麼 工 作

帕蘭卡：丁雲，我問你，你想不想家？
Palanka: Dīng Yún, wǒ wèn nǐ, nǐ xiǎng bu xiǎng jiā?

丁　雲：想。我很想爸爸，媽媽。
Ding Yun: Xiǎng. Wǒ hěn xiǎng bàba, māma.

帕蘭卡：不想你男朋友嗎？
Palanka: Bù xiǎng nǐ nán péngyou ma?

丁　雲：也想。
Ding Yun: Yě xiǎng.

帕蘭卡：他作什麼工作？
Palanka: Tā zuò shénme gōngzuò?

丁　雲：他是大夫。
Ding Yun: Tā shì dàifu.

(144, 145)

帕蘭卡：你有沒有妹妹？
Palanka: Nǐ yǒu mei yǒu mèimei?

丁　雲：我沒有妹妹，我有姐姐。
Ding Yun: Wǒ méi yǒu mèimei, wǒ yǒu jiějie.

帕蘭卡：你姐姐在哪兒工作？
Palanka: Nǐ jiějie zài nǎr gōngzuò?

丁　雲：她在銀行工作，她愛人在書店工作。
Ding Yun: Tā zài yínháng gōngzuò, tā àiren zài shūdiàn gōngzuò.

帕蘭卡：她有孩子嗎？
Palanka: Tā yǒu háizi ma?

丁　雲：有。他們常常給我寫信，我也常常給他們寫信。
Ding Yun: Yǒu. Tāmen chángcháng gěi wǒ xiě xìn, wǒ yě chángcháng gěi tāmen xiě xìn.

帕蘭卡：他們好嗎？
Palanka: Tāmen hǎo ma?

丁　雲：他們都很好。我告訴姐姐：你是我的好朋友。我姐姐
Ding Yun: Tāmen dōu hěn hǎo. Wǒ gàosu jiějie: nǐ shì wǒ de hǎo péngyou. Wǒ jiějie

　　　　問你好。
　　　　wèn nǐ hǎo.

帕蘭卡：謝謝。問他們好。
Palanka: Xièxie. Wèn tāmen hǎo.

二、生　詞

1.作	zuò	to do
2.工作	gōngzuò	to work, work
3.想	xiǎng	to want, to think, to miss
4.家	jiā	family, home, house
5.有	yǒu	to have, there be
6.沒*	méi	not, no
7.妹妹	mèimei	younger sister
8.姐姐	jiějie	elder sister
9.銀行	yínháng	bank
10.愛人	àiren	husband or wife
11.書店	shūdiàn	bookstore
12.孩子	háizi	child
13.給	gěi	to, for, to give
14.寫	xiě	to write
15.信	xìn	letter
16.告訴	gàosu	to tell

補 充 詞

1.職員	zhíyuán	office worker, staff member
2.工程師	gōngchéngshī	engineer
3.經理	jīnglǐ	manager, director

*沒 is interchangeable with 没

4.公司　　　　　　gōngsī　　　　　　company

三、閱讀短文

　　帕蘭卡家有爸爸、媽媽、哥哥和姐姐。她爸爸是教授，在外語學院工作。她媽媽是大夫。他們都很忙。

　　帕蘭卡沒有弟弟，也沒有妹妹，她有哥哥和姐姐。他哥哥是公司的職員。他不在家住，我們不認識他。她哥哥的愛人現在沒有工作。他們的孩子叫保爾 (Bǎo'ěr)。

　　帕蘭卡的姐姐是學生，現在在法國(Fǎguó, France)學習。帕蘭卡很想姐姐，她常給姐姐寫信。姐姐常常給她買法語書和畫報。

四、注釋 Notes

1. "你想不想家？"

The word "家" here refers to members of the family.

2. "想。""也想。"

"想。" and "也想。" are both elliptical sentences in which the subject "我" and the objects "家" and "男朋友" are respectively understood.

3. "不想你男朋友嗎？"

"Don't you miss your boy friend?"

In a question with the interrogative particle "嗎", the predicative verb may be made negative to imply that an answer in the affirmative is expected.

4. "她愛人在書店工作。"

"Her husband works in a bookstore."

In Chinese, the word "愛人" may refer to either "husband" or "wife".

5. "他們常常給我寫信。"

"They often write to me."

In colloquial speech "常" often takes the form of "常常", but the negative form remains "不常".

6. "我姐姐問你好。"

"My elder sister wished to be remembered to you." or "My elder sister sends you her love."

"問他們好"

"Please remember me to them." or "Give them my love."

"問…好" is an expression used to ask someone to give one's love or send one's best regards to a third person. "他問你好" is used by the speaker when he gives the regards of a third person to the person spoken to. "他問她好" is used when a third person asks the person spoken to to give his respects to another person. When the speaker asks the person spoken to to say hello to a third person, the subject "I" can be omitted. E.g. "（我）問他們好".

　　　　　　　　(147, 148, 149)

五、替換與擴展 Substitution and Extension

㈠

1. 你有<u>漢語詞典</u>嗎?
   我有漢語詞典。
   你現在用不用?
   我現在不用。

中國地圖
英語書
車
筆

2. 他有沒有<u>妹妹</u>?
   他沒有妹妹。
   那是誰?
   那是他<u>姐姐</u>。

姐姐,	妹妹
弟弟,	哥哥
妹妹,	女朋友
愛人,	朋友
孩子,	姐姐的孩子

3. 你爸爸作什麼工作?
   他是<u>大夫</u>。
   他好嗎?
   謝謝你,他很好。

老師	敎授˙
職員˙	經理˙
工程師˙	

4. 您在哪兒工作?
   我在<u>銀行</u>工作。
   您忙不忙?
   我很忙。

外語學院
書店
商店
公司‧

5. 你在哪兒<u>學習</u>?
   我在<u>外語學院</u><u>學習</u>。

住,	學生宿舍
看書,	家
寫信,	家

6. 你常常給<u>他</u>寫信嗎?
   我常常給他寫信。

你朋友	你姐姐
你爸爸	謝先生
你愛人	

(二)

1. Asking about occupation

   A：你好! 我們認識一下兒,
      我叫 _____ 。

   B：我叫 _____ 。我是職員‧。
      請問, 你作什麼工作?

   A：我是學生。

   B：你在哪兒學習?

— 113 —

A：我在外語學院學習。

           *   *   *

A：喂，商先生！

B：啊，是你，丁先生，你好！

A：你好。你現在在哪兒工作？

B：我在銀行工作，你呢？

A：我在公司工作。你忙不忙？

B：不忙。你孩子好嗎？

A：很好。問你愛人好。

B：謝謝。再見！

A：再見！

2. Introducing people to each other

A：我給你們介紹一下兒。

這是我們公司的丁經理，

這是銀行的商先生

B：您好！

C：您好！

3. Sending someone your love or kind regards

A：你哥哥常給你寫信嗎？

B：他常給我寫信。他也問你好。

A：謝謝。

           *   *   *

A：你爸爸好嗎？

B：很好，謝謝。

A：我爸爸問他好。

B：謝謝。

＊　　　＊　　　＊

A：問你愛人好。再見!

B：謝謝，再見!

＊　　　＊　　　＊

學生登記表

Xuesheng Dengji Biao

Registration Form for Students

姓名 Name	性別 Sex	年齡 Age	國籍 Nationality	住址 Address
丁　雲	女	22	中　國	學生宿舍423號

六、語法 Grammar

1. "有" sentences

A "有" sentence is one in which the verb "有", which denotes posses-sion, functions as the main element of the predicate. Such a sentence is made negative by preceding "有" with "沒" (and never with "不"). "有沒有 …" is used to build an affirmative-negative question with "有".

(152, 153, 154)

Nouns or pronouns	Verbs	Nouns	Particle
老師	有	中國地圖。	
我	沒有	漢語詞典。	
他	有	女朋友	嗎？
他家	有沒有	車？	

2. Prepositional constructions

The preposition " 在 " or " 給 " together with its object forms a prepositional construction, which is often placed before verbs as an adverbial
adjunct.

Nouns or pronouns	Adverbs	Prepositional constructions	Verbs	Nouns	Particle
他		在書店	買	書。	
她愛人	不	在銀行	工作。		
我朋友	也	在外語學院	學習。		
他們	常	給你	寫	信	嗎？
她		給我們	介紹	中國。	

Points to be noted:

(1) The prepositional construction " 在 … " or " 給 … " never comes
after the verb it qualifies and it is incorrect to say "他工作在銀行".

(2)   The object of the preposition "在" is usually a word or phrase denoting a place while the object of the preposition "給" is often the receiver of the action expressed by the verb that follows.

(3)   In a negative sentence, the adverb "不" usually goes before the prepositional construction.

七、練習 Exercises

1.   Read out the following phrases and make sentences with them:

(1)   在中國學習　在家寫信

在學院看書　在書店買書

(2)   給他們介紹　給老師寫信

給誰寫信　給姐姐買畫報

給留學生還書

(3)   問她好　問他們好　問你朋友好

問老師好　問古波好

2.   Change the following to affirmative-negative questions and answer them in the negative:

Example　她有紙。

→她有沒有紙？

她沒有紙。

(1)   你朋友有法語詞典。

(2)   他們有中國雜誌。(zázhì or "magazine", see p. 125)

　　　　　　　　(155, 156, 157)

(3) 古波有漢語書。

(4) 他有好筆。

(5) 帕蘭卡有中國朋友。

(6) 留學生有外語畫報。

3. Put in the preposition "在" or "給" in the following sentences:

(1) 他＿書店買書。

(2) 我＿朋友買畫報。

(3) 她姐姐＿中國學習。

(4) 他朋友不＿商店工作。

(5) 丁雲＿他們介紹北京。(Běijīng)

(6) 她不常＿我寫信。

(7) 她常常＿宿舍喝茶。

4. Make up a dialogue with a fellow student of yours, using the hints given:

(1) 你叫什麼名字?

(2) 你是哪國人?

(3) 你作什麼工作?

(4) 你住哪兒?

(5) 你有沒有哥哥?

(6) 他是不是職員˙?

(7) 他在哪兒工作?

(8) 他有孩子嗎?

(9) 孩子在哪兒學習?

(10) 他愛人工作不工作?

(11) 她作什麼工作?

(12) 她在不在這兒?

5. Say something about your family after the fashion of the Reading Text, and then write it out.

八、語音語調 Pronunciation and Intonation

1. Word stress (2)

When a noun is formed of reduplicated characters the first character receives a strong stress and the second one is pronounced in the neutral tone. E.g.

爸爸　姐姐　哥哥

媽媽　妹妹　弟弟

2. Exercises

(1) Read out the following dissyllabic words, paying attention to the main stress and weak stress:

the 1st tone + the neutral tone:

媽媽　哥哥　她們　他們

the 2nd tone + the neutral tone:

朋友　學生　什麼　名字

the 3rd tone + the neutral tone:

姐姐　你們　我們

the 4th tone + the neutral tone:

妹妹　弟弟　愛人　告訴

(2)　Read out the following words and expressions, paying attention to the pronunciation of j, q and x:

jiā　（家）：他家　誰家　想家　在家

jiě　（姐）：姐姐　小姐

qǐng　（請）：請問　請進　請坐　請看

xué　（學）：學習　學院　學生

Read out the following short passage:

丁雲的姐姐在銀行工作。她姐姐也學習英語。她很想丁雲，常給丁雲寫信。她問帕蘭卡好。

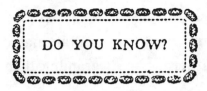

Chinese Forms of Address for Different Family Relationships

Chinese forms of address for the various family relationships are very complicated.   The following diagram will show you how members of a Chinese family call each other.   (See next page.)

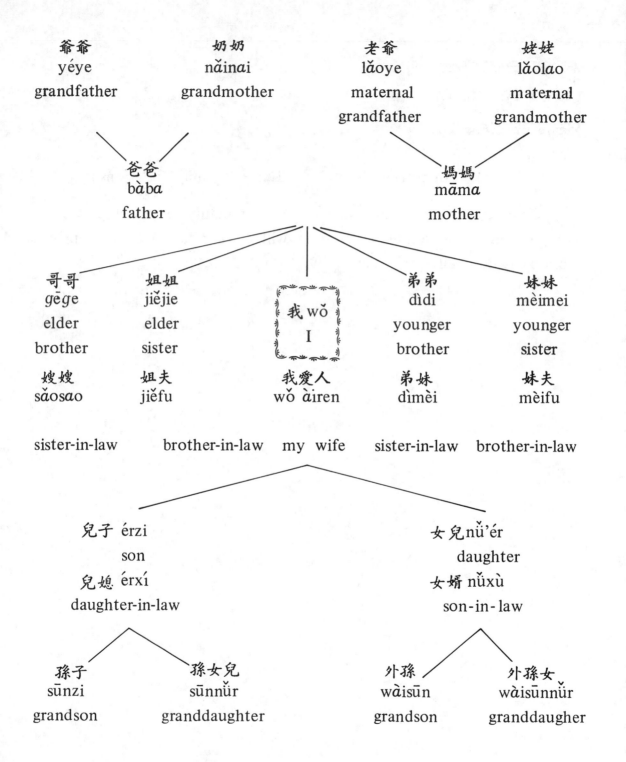

第十五課

一、課 文

中文系有多少學生

帕蘭卡：這是我們中文系。
Palanka: Zhè shì wǒmen Zhōngwén xì.

丁　雲：中文系有多少學生？
Ding Yun: Zhōngwén xì yǒu duōshao xuésheng?

古　波：我們系有九十八個學生。
Gubo: Wǒmen xì yǒu jiǔshibāge xuésheng.

丁　雲：有幾個中國老師？
Ding Yun; Yǒu jǐge Zhōngguó lǎoshī?

帕蘭卡：有三個中國老師。王老師教我們語法和漢字。
Palanka: Yǒu sānge Zhōngguó lǎoshī. Wáng Lǎoshī jiāo wǒmen yǔfǎ hé Hànzì.

古　波：我和帕蘭卡還有一個中國老師。
Gubo: Wǒ hé Pàlánkǎ hái yǒu yíge Zhōngguó lǎoshī.

(165, 166)

丁　雲：誰？
Ding Yun: Shéi?

古　波：丁老師，她敎我們口語。
Gubo: Dīng Lǎoshī, tā jiāo wǒmen kǒuyǔ.

丁　雲：不敢當。你們是我的英語老師。
Ding Yun: Bù gǎndāng. Nǐmen shì wǒ de Yīngyǔ lǎoshī.

帕蘭卡：我們互相學習。
Palanka: Wǒmen hùxiāng xuéxí.

古　波：這是我們的新閱覽室。我們常在閱覽室看畫報和雜誌。
Gubo: Zhè shì wǒmen de xīn yuèlǎnshì. Wǒmen cháng zài yuèlǎnshì kàn huàbào hé zázhì.

丁　雲：閱覽室有中文雜誌嗎？
Ding Yun: Yuèlǎnshì yǒu Zhōngwén zázhì ma?

帕蘭卡：有，閱覽室有中文雜誌、中文報，還有七本漢語詞典。
Palanka: Yǒu, yuèlǎnshì yǒu Zhōngwén zázhì, Zhōngwén bào, hái yǒu qīběn Hànyǔ cídiǎn.

丁　雲：圖書館在哪兒？
Ding Yun: Túshūguǎn zài nǎr?

古　波：在那兒。
Gubo: Zài nàr.

二、生　詞

1.中文	Zhōngwén	Chinese (language)
2.系	xì	department

(166, 167)
— 124 —

3.個	gè	a measure word
4.幾	jǐ	how many, how much, several
5.教	jiāo	to teach
6.語法	yǔfǎ	grammar
7.漢字	Hànzì	Chinese character
字	zì	character
8.還	hái	else, in addition, still
9.口語	kǒuyǔ	spoken language
10.不敢當	bù gǎndāng	I don't really deserve it, you flatter me
11.互相	hùxiāng	each other, mutually
12.新	xīn	new
13.閱覽室	yuèlǎnshì	reading-room
14.雜誌	zázhì	magazine
15.報	bào	newspaper
16.本	běn	a measure word
17.圖書館	túshūguǎn	library
18.那兒	nàr	there

專　名

王	Wáng	a surname

補　充　詞

1.班　　　　　bān　　　　　class, squad
2.教室　　　　jiàoshì　　　　classroom
3.實驗室　　　shíyànshì　　　laboratory
4.借　　　　　jiè　　　　　　to borrow, to lend
5.生詞　　　　shēngcí　　　　new word

三、閱讀短文

　　我們學院有八個系。我在中文系學習漢語。我們班有十五個學生——七個男學生，八個女學生。中國老師教我們語法和口語。

　　我們系有一個閱覽室。那兒有英文雜誌和英文畫報，也有中文雜誌和中文報。我們常常在閱覽室看書。

　　我們學院還有一個圖書館。我常常去圖書館借中文書。中國老師常給我們介紹新書。

　　我們學院沒有宿舍，我在學生城 (chéng, city, town)住。我有一個好朋友，他叫古波。古波也住那兒。他和帕蘭卡都在我們班。

四、注釋 Notes

1. "這是我們中文系"

"中文系" is the short form for "the Chinese Language and Literature Department".

Both "漢語" and "中文" refer to the language of China's Han nationality, the chief language spoken and written in China. In practical use, however, the two terms have slightly different points of emphasis. "漢語" usually refers to Chinese as it is spoken, and "中文", on the other hand, refers to the written language of the Han nationality and its literature. Here are some common expressions that will show you the difference in usage: "學習漢語", "說漢語", "中文畫報" and "中文系".

The same is true of "英語" and "英文", "法語" and "法文".

2. "中文系有多少學生?"

"How many students are there in the Chinese Language and Literature Department?"

"閱覽室有中文雜誌嗎?"

"Are there any Chinese language magazines in the reading room?"

Besides denoting possession, the verb "有" also indicates existence. In a sentence with "有" indicating existence, the noun that precedes the verb, denoting either a collective or a place, is the subject of the sentence. "沒有" is used to make the sentence negative, e.g. "閱覽室沒有中文雜誌".

3. "有幾個中國老師?"

"幾" and "多少" are both used to ask about numbers. "幾" is usually used with respect to a number smaller than ten. "多少" is used for any number.

There must be a measure word between "幾" and the noun it qualifies. "多少" is used with or without a measure word. E.g.

你有多少（本）英文雜誌?

她認識幾個中國朋友？

4. "我和帕蘭卡還有一個中國老師。"

The use of the adverb "還" (1) is "in addition to" or "besides". E.g.

王老師教語法，還教口語。

我認識那個留學生，還常常去宿舍看他。 [See p. 143(3)]

5. "誰？"

"誰？" here is an elliptical question, meaning "那個中國老師是誰？" Other interrogative pronouns such as "什麼", "哪兒" and "多少" can also be used elliptically if the context or situation leaves no room for misunderstanding.

Note that "誰" has two pronunciations: "shéi" and "shúi". The former is preferred in colloquial speech.

6. "不敢當。你們是我的英語老師。"

"不敢當", meaning "I don't really deserve it", is used in reply to a complimentary remark from the person spoken to.

7. "我們互相學習。"

"Let's learn from each other."

五、替換與擴展　Substitution and Extension

(一)

1. 你在中文系學習嗎？
   我在中文系學習。
   你們系有幾個老師？
   我們系有十個老師。

法國學生	教室
留學生	班
教授	

2. 你去哪兒?
　我去外語學院。
　你們學院有幾個系?
　我們學院有五個系。

圖書館,	1
閱覽室,	6
實驗室*,	4

3. 圖書館有多少本漢語詞典?
　有二十本漢語詞典。
　你常去圖書館借*書嗎?
　我常去圖書館借書。

中文書,	95
語法書,	40
口語書,	37

4. 你有多少中文畫報?
　我有十二本中文畫報,
　我還有英文畫報。

中文雜誌,	18,	英文雜誌
英文書,	70,	中文書
法語詞典,	3,	漢語詞典

5. 誰教你們語法?
　王老師教我們語法。
　他教不教你們漢字?
　他也教我們漢字。

口語
漢語
生詞*

6. 你還他什麼?
　我還他報。

雜誌	筆
畫報	書

(二)

1. Talking about your family

    A：你家有幾個人？

    B：我家有五個人：爸爸、媽媽、我愛人，還有一個孩子。

    A：你愛人也工作嗎？

    B：她也工作，她在圖書館工作。你有幾個孩子？

    A：我有三個孩子。他們都是學生。

2. Talking about your studies

    A：你是不是中文系的學生？

    B：我是中文系的學生。

    A：幾個中國老師教你們？

    B：三個中國老師教我們。

    A：中國老師教你們什麼？

    B：他們教我們語法和口語。

    A：你常寫漢字嗎？

    B：我常寫漢字。

    A：你現在認識多少漢字？

    B：我現在認識九十個漢字。

3. Making a reply to a complimentary remark from the person spoken to

    A：你的英語很好，請多 (duō, many, much, more) 幫助 (bāngzhu, to help) 我。

    B：不敢當，我們互相學習。

(173, 174, 175)   — 130 —

4. Buying books

A：請問，有漢語語法書嗎？

B：有。你買幾本？

A：我買一本。有沒有中文雜誌？

B：沒有。

* * *

人民日報

RENMIN RIBAO

(See p. 247)

人民圣书   光明日報

六、語法　Grammar

1. Numeration for numbers under 100

In Chinese, the decimal system is used for numeration.

一	二	三	四	五
六	七	八	九	十
十一	十二	十三	十四	十五
十六	十七	十八	十九	二十
二十一	....		二十九	三十
....				九十九

(175, 176, 177)

2. Numeral-measure words as attributives

In modern Chinese, a numeral alone cannot function as an attributive but must be combined with a measure word inserted between the numeral and the noun it modifies. E.g.

他們有一個孩子。

我買十二本中文書。

他教五十個學生。

In Chinese, every noun as a rule has its specific measure word and can't go freely with others. In this lesson we only deal with the measure words "個" and "本". Of all the measure words "個" is the most extensively used. It can be placed before a noun denoting a person, thing or unit. "本" is placed before nouns denoting books and such like. E.g.

一個	老師　學生　大夫　人　朋友　哥哥　弟弟 姐姐　妹妹　孩子　學院　系　圖書館　閱覽室 宿舍　食堂　書店　銀行
一本	書　雜誌　畫報　詞典

Points to be noted:

(1) Chinese nouns have no number. A noun may be either singular or plural without any change of form.

(2) Whether a noun denotes one person or thing or more than one is shown mainly by other members of the sentence such as attributives (made of numeral-measure words, demonstrative pronouns or adjectives).

3. Sentences with a predicate verb taking two objects

Some verbs can take two objects: an indirect object (usually referring to a person) and a direct object (usually referring to a thing), with the former preceding the latter.

Nouns or pronouns	Verbs	Nouns or pronouns (referring to persons)	Nouns (referring to things)
王老師 我 他 帕蘭卡	教 還 告訴 問	我們 丁雲 我 古波	語法。 詞典。 他的名字。 一個漢字。

Note that some but not all Chinese verbs can take two objects; there are only a small number that can. Sentences such as "他買我一本書" and "我介紹他我的朋友" are incorrect. Chinese idiom requires that the indirect objects "我" and "他" be preceded by the preposition "給". That is why it is correct to say "他給我買一本書" and "我給他介紹我的朋友".

七、練習 Exercises

1. Read out the following phrases and make sentences with them:

中文系　英文系　法文系　外語系

中文書　英文書　法文書　外文書

中文雜誌　中文畫報　漢語詞典

— 133 —

英文雜誌　英文畫報　英語詞典

法文雜誌　法文畫報　法語詞典

外文雜誌　外文畫報　外語詞典

2. Read the following numbers, then write them out in Chinese characters:

    10   54   32   61

    40   17   99   82

3. Do the following sums orally with a fellow student of yours:

Example　　1 + 2

　　　　　→一加 (jiā, plus) 二是幾?

　　　　　一加二是三。

(1) 4 + 6　　　(2) 21 + 18　　　(3) 37 + 3

(2) 50 + 20　　(5) 68 + 27

Example　　20 − 3

　　　　　→二十減 (jiǎn, minus) 三是多少?

　　　　　二十減三是十七。

(1) 85 − 4　　(2) 48 − 18　　(3) 90 − 32

(4) 6 − 1　　(5) 79 − 69

4. Try to say the following multiplication formulas:

Example　一二得 (dé, to get) 二　　(1 × 2 = 2)

　　　　　二三得六　　　　　(2 × 3 = 6)

(180, 181)　　　　　　　　　　− 134 −

四七二十八　　（ 4 × 7 = 28 ）

(1) 一六 _____

(2) 六七 _____

(3) 三八 _____

(4) 四九 _____

(5) 七七 _____

(6) 五八 _____

(7) 八九 _____

(8) 九九 _____

5. Fill in the blanks with measure words, and then ask questions using " 多少 " or " 幾 ":

Example　　我有一____中國朋友。

　　　　　　→我有一個中國朋友。

　　　　　　你有幾個中國朋友？

(1) 三 ____ 老師教我們。

(2) 他去書店買一 ____ 語法書。

(3) 我們醫院有五十 ____ 大夫。

(4) 閱覽室有八十七 ____ 畫報。

(5) 這兒有一 ____ 銀行。

6. Answer the following questions:

(1) 誰教古波語法？

(181, 182)

(2) 丁雲是不是老師? 她教他們什麼?

(3) 他們教丁雲什麼?

(4) 你們班有幾個老師?

(5) 誰教你們語法?

(6) 中國老師教你們什麼?

(7) 你問老師什麼?

(8) 你問誰生詞*?

八、語音語調　Pronunciation and Intonation

1. Word stress (3)

(1) When a numeral is combined with a measure word, the numeral generally has a strong stress and the measure word is pronounced with a weak stress. E.g.

三個　（老師）　　七本　（詞典）

六個　（學生）　　四本　（畫報）

五個　（大夫）　　九本　（雜誌）

(2) The numeral "十", when standing alone, is uttered with a strong stress. When "十" is combined with other numerals, it is not stressed if it forms the first element, as in "十二", but it is stressed when it is the second element, as in "三十". When "十" is followed by a measure word, it is pronounced with a weak stress, as in "三十個", "四十本". When "十" is sandwiched between other numerals it is also pronounced with a weak stress, as in "九十三個".

(182, 183)

2. The changes of tones of " 一 ":

The word " 一 " is normally pronounced in the 1st tone. When " 一 " is followed by a syllable in the 4th tone, or by a syllable in the neutral tone transformed from the 4th tone, it is pronounced in the 2nd tone, as in " 一個 ". If " 一 " is followed by a syllable in tones other than those mentioned above, it is pronounced in the 4th tone, e.g. " 一本 ".

3. Exercises

(1) Read aloud the following numerals, paying attention to the pronunciation of " 十 ":

六　　七　　八　　九　　十

十一　十二　十三　十四　十五

二十　三十　四十　五十　六十

七十　八十　二十一　三十二

七十三　八十四　九十五　四十個

五十個　六十個　七十個　八十個

二十二本　七十四本　八十五本

六十三本　九十九本　五十一本

(2) Read aloud the following words and expressions containing the sounds z, c and s, paying attention to their pronunciation and tone:

z: 在　坐　再見　漢字　名字

c: 詞典　三層　生詞

s: 四個　三十　告訴　宿舍

　　　　　　　　(184, 185)

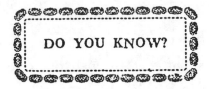

Education in China

China's education is divided into three stages: primary school, secondary or middle school and college or university. According to China's present educational system, the length of schooling is five years for primary school, six years for secondary or middle school (three years for junior middle school and three years for senior middle school), four years for college (five years for certain subjects). There are also secondary vocational or technical schools (usually three years) and technical colleges (usually two or three years). We have universities (大學) such as "Beijing University", "Fudan University". We àlso have institutions of higher learning specialized in one subject or study known as " 學院 " (colleges or institutes) such as "Beijing Engineering Institute", "Beijing Foreign Languages Institute".

The various departments in a university or an institute are known in China as " 系 " each of which consists of a number of specialities.

第 十 六 課

一、課 文

這 條 裙 子 是 新 的

古　波：帕蘭卡，王老師給我們兩張票。
Gubo:　Pàlánkǎ, Wáng Lǎoshī gěi wǒmen liǎng zhāng piào.

帕蘭卡：什麼票？
Palanka:　Shénme piào?

古　波：京劇票。我們晚上去看京劇。
Gubo:　Jīngjù piào. Wǒmen wǎnshang qù kàn jīngjù.

帕蘭卡：太好了。
Palanka:　Tài hǎo le.

古　波：我們從哪兒去？
Gubo:　Wǒmen cóng nǎr qù?

帕蘭卡：從我家去。
Palanka:　Cóng wǒ jiā qù.

(189, 190)

媽　媽：你找什麼？
Mama: Nǐ zhǎo shénme?

帕蘭卡：我找一條裙子。我和古波晚上看京劇。
Palanka: Wǒ zhǎo yìtiáo qúnzi. Wǒ hé Gǔbō wǎnshang kàn jīngjù.

媽　媽：你的裙子在我這兒。是這條嗎？
Mama: Nǐ de qúnzi zài wǒ zhèr. Shì zhè tiáo ma?

帕蘭卡：這條裙子不是我的，這是姐姐的。
Palanka: Zhè tiáo qúnzi bú shì wǒ de, zhè shì jiějie de.

媽　媽：那兒還有兩條。
Mama: Nàr hái yǒu liǎngtiáo.

帕蘭卡：也不是。那都是舊的。
Palanka: Yě bú shì. Nà dōu shì jiù de.

媽　媽：這條裙子是新的，是不是這條？
Mama: Zhè tiáo qúnzi shì xīn de, shì bu shì zhè tiáo?

帕蘭卡：對了，是這條。媽媽，我穿哪件襯衫？
Palanka: Duì le, shì zhè tiáo. Māma, wǒ chuān nǎ jiàn chènshān?

媽　媽：那件綠的很好。
Mama: Nàjiàn lǜ de hěn hǎo.

帕蘭卡：不，那件太大，我穿白襯衫。
Palanka: Bù, nàjiàn tài dà, wǒ chuān bái chènshān.

二、生　詞

1. 條　　　tiáo　　　a measure word

2. 裙子　　qúnzi　　skirt

3. 兩　　　liǎng　　two

4. 張　　　zhāng　　a measure word, piece

5. 票　　　piào　　ticket

6. 京劇　　jīngjù　　Beijing opera

7. 晚上　　wǎnshang　evening

8. 太　　　tài　　　too, too much

9. 從　　　cóng　　from

10. 找　　　zhǎo　　to look for, to call on (a person)

11. 這兒　　zhèr　　here

12. 舊　　　jiù　　　old

13. 穿　　　chuān　　to put on, to wear

14. 件　　　jiàn　　a measure word

15. 襯衫　　chènshān　shirt, blouse

16. 綠　　　lǜ　　　green

17. 大　　　dà　　　big, large

18. 白　　　bái　　white

補 充 詞

1. 藍　　　　　lán　　　　　blue
2. 上衣　　　　shàngyī　　　upper outer garment, jacket
3. 褲子　　　　kùzi　　　　trousers
4. 大衣　　　　dàyī　　　　overcoat, topcoat
5. 黑　　　　　hēi　　　　black, dark
6. 劇場　　　　jùchǎng　　　theatre
7. 座位　　　　zuòwèi　　　seat

三、閱讀短文

　　帕蘭卡問媽媽："晚上您用不用車？"媽媽說："不用。你去哪兒？"帕蘭卡告訴媽媽，王老師給他們兩張京劇票，她和古波晚上去看京劇。

　　晚上，他們從帕蘭卡那兒去劇場。帕蘭卡穿一件新襯衫和一條新裙子，襯衫是白的，裙子是綠的。古波穿一件黑上衣，他的上衣也是新的。

　　這個劇場很大。帕蘭卡問古波："我們的座位在哪兒？"古波說："那兩個座位是我們的。你看，王老師在那兒。那兒還有兩個中國留學生。"

四、注釋 Notes

1. "王老師給我們兩張票。"

"給" is here a verb.

Both "二" and "兩" mean "2". When "2" comes before a measure word (or before a noun which needs no measure word before it), "兩" is used instead of "二", as in "兩張票", "兩條裙子". But in numbers larger than ten (12, 20, 22, 32, etc.), "二" is used irrespective of whether it is followed by a measure word, as in "十二個老師".

The measure word "張" is used to apply to paper or anything having a smooth surface or top like paper, as in "一張報", "一張紙" or "一張桌子 (zhuōzi, table)".

2. "太好了。"

"太好了" is an expression used to show satisfaction or admiration. The word "太" signifies a very high degree of such sentiments.

Note that the adverb "太" is more often than not used to signify "excess" or something that goes beyond the accepted standard. "這條裙子太大" means "This skirt is much too big for me". "不太", the negative form of "太", means about the same as "不很".

3. "這條裙子不是我的。"

When the demonstrative pronoun "這" or "那" functions as an attributive, the noun it qualifies also takes a measure word before it, e.g. "那張票", "這件襯衫".

4. "是這條嗎？" "那兒還有兩條。"

"是這條嗎？" means "Is this the skirt you are looking for?" "那兒還有兩條" means "There are two more skirts there." When a demonstrative pronoun plus a measure word or a numeral plus a measure word functions as an attributive, the noun it qualifies can be understood if the context leaves no room for doubt. E.g.

— 143 —   (193, 194, 195)

我有兩本中文書，一本（書）是新的，

一本（書）是舊的。

五、替換與擴展　Substitution and Extension

（一）

1. 這張票是你的嗎?
   這張票不是我的，是她的。
   那張票也是她的嗎?
   那張票也是她的。

地圖	（張）
裙子	（條）
襯衫	（件）
詞典	（本）
本子*	（個）

2. 你有幾本雜誌?
   我有一本。
   那兩本雜誌是誰的?
   那兩本雜誌都是古波的。

老師
他們
我哥哥
圖書館

3. 你的襯衫是不是新的?
   我的襯衫不是新的，是舊的。

綠，	白
白，	藍*

4. 他爸爸給他什麼?
   他爸爸給他兩本書。

十二本雜誌	一件上衣*
兩件襯衫	兩條褲子*

(195, 196)

5. 你晚上去不去商店？

　我去商店。

　你從哪兒去？

　我從家去。

|宿舍|
|圖書館|
|銀行|
|書店|

6. 你從書店來嗎？

　不，我從朋友那兒來。

|古波的宿舍|
|謝先生那兒|
|帕蘭卡家|

㈡

1. Looking for something

　A：喂，你找什麼？

　B：我找我的筆。

　A：你的筆是新的嗎？

　B：不是新的，是舊的。

　A˚：是不是黑的？

　B：對了，在哪兒？

　A：在那兒。

　B：謝謝你。

2. Seeing a guest off

　A：這是您的大衣*。

　B：這不是我的，我的大衣*是藍*的。

　A：是這件嗎？

B：對了，謝謝您，再見！

A：再見！

3. Talking about books

A：這是什麼書？

B：這是漢語語法書。

A：這本書是英文的嗎？

B：不是英文的，是法文的。

A：你有英文的嗎？

B：我沒有。

A：我去書店買一本英文的。

*　　　*　　　*

京劇票 jīngjù piaò
Beijing opera Ticket

六、語法　Grammar

1. "是" sentences type (2)

A pronoun, an adjective or a noun plus the structural particle "的" forms what is called a "的" construction. In a sentence a "的" construction does the same work as a noun and can stand by itself. This type of construction often forms part of a "是" sentence. E.g.

哪本畫報是你的？

那條裙子是舊的，你有新的嗎？

我們家的車是綠的，他們家的車是藍的。

我有英文的漢語語法書，我去買一本法文的。

那個老師是你們系的嗎？

2. Object of the preposition "從"

The object of the preposition "從" is usually a word or phrase denoting place or time. In the case of a noun or pronoun not indicating place, "這兒" or "那兒" must be added to it before it becomes an object of the preposition "從", forming a prepositional construction qualifying the predicative verb. E.g.

我從朋友那兒來。

他從我這兒去書店。

The same is true of the object of the preposition "在" as well as the objects of the verbs "來", "去" and "在" when they denote places. E.g.

你弟弟在我這兒看雜誌。

她去張大夫那兒。

朋友們常常來我這兒。

我的筆在誰那兒？

我的筆在古波那兒。

七、練習 Exercises

1. Read out the following phrases and make sentences with them:

新詞典　新書　新畫報　新地圖

新圖書館　舊宿舍　舊筆　舊車

舊雜誌　舊襯衫　綠裙子　白紙

大商店　大書店　大詞典

2. Write out the following numerals in Chinese characters, and then fill in each blank with an appropriate measure word:

  2 ＿＿＿ 書店　　　　20 ＿＿＿ 裙子

12 ＿＿＿ 襯衫　　　　 2 ＿＿＿ 地圖

92 ＿＿＿ 票　　　　22 ＿＿＿ 雜誌

 7 ＿＿＿ 大夫　　　　 1 ＿＿＿ 孩子

3. Change the following to sentences with "的" construction as the object of the verb "是", paying special attention to the use of measure words:

Example　　這是我的書。

→這本書是我的。

(1) 這是綠襯衫。

(2) 那是中文畫報。

(3) 這是閱覽室的雜誌。

(4) 那是妹妹的裙子。

(5) 這是我們老師的地圖。

(6) 那是我們學院的宿舍。

4. Put in an appropriate preposition in each of the following sentences:

(1) 古波 ＿＿＿ 宿舍寫漢字。

(2) 她 ＿＿＿ 丁雲那兒來。

(3) 我 ＿＿＿ 我朋友買一本書。

(4) 我們 ＿＿＿ 宿舍去商店。

(5) 你 ＿＿＿ 哪兒看京劇?

(6) 他 ＿＿＿ 圖書館來這兒。

5. Change the following to questions with an interrogative pronoun, substituting suitable interrogative pronouns for the underlined words or phrases:

(1) 她給<u>妹妹</u>一條裙子。

(2) 他愛人從<u>銀行</u>來。

(3) 王老師教他們<u>漢語</u>。

(4) 我穿<u>綠</u>襯衫。

(5) 他常常在<u>他朋友那兒</u>喝茶。

(6) 那個女學生從圖書館去<u>書店</u>。

(7) 他給<u>我</u>一本畫報。

(8) 那本書的名字叫《<u>漢語口語</u>》。

6. Play games with fellow students of yours:

Student A reads aloud the two lines from the nursery rhyme given below, Student B changes "一個青蛙" to "兩個青蛙", Student C changes "兩個青蛙" to "三個青蛙" and so on. Note that the number of mouths, eyes and legs must increase as the number of frogs increases.

A：一個青蛙 (qīngwā, frog) 一張嘴 (zuǐ, mouth)

兩個眼睛 (yǎnjing, eye) 四條腿 (tuǐ, leg)

B：兩個青蛙……

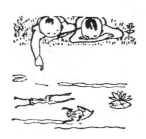

八、語音語調　Pronunciation and Intonation

1. Word stress (4)

The first syllable of a dissyllable formed with the suffix "子" is stressed, and "子" is pronounced in the neutral tone. E.g.

裙子　褲子　孩子　本子

In "的" constructions formed of the structural particle "的" and a noun, a pronoun or an adjective, "的" is always pronounced in the neutral tone. E.g.

新的　舊的　綠的　他的　姐姐的

2. Exercises

Read aloud the following dissyllabic words, paying attention to the changes of the 3rd tone and word stress:

老師　兩張　北京
兩條　五層　
語法　口語　九本
請問　九號　五件
晚上　本子　姐姐

Read aloud the following proverbs:

Zhòng zhì chéng chéng.　(Unity of will is an impregnable
眾　志　成　城。　　stronghold.)

Shībài shì chénggōng zhī mǔ.　(Failure is the mother of
失敗　是　成功　之　母。　success.)

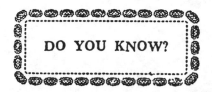

Beijing Opera

Beijing opera is a form of traditional Chinese drama with a history of about 150 years. It took shape in Beijing and became popular throughout the country. It is a comprehensive expression of the traditional Chinese drama, music, dance, boxing and fencing, and it has always been loved by the Chinese people.

Beijing opera is characterized by its symbolic actions, giving full play to the various artistic mediums of singing, acting, recitation and acrobatics accompanied by the rhythmic beats of gongs and drums. It has thus formed a perfect artistic system of its own.

第 十 七 課

一、課 文

現 在 幾 點

帕蘭卡：你從哪兒來？
Palanka: Nǐ cóng nǎr lái?

古　波：我從食堂來。現在幾點？
Gubo: Wǒ cóng shítáng lái. Xiànzài jǐdiǎn?

帕蘭卡：差五分兩點。
Palanka: Chà wǔfēn liǎngdiǎn.

古　波：我兩點一刻上課。
Gubo: Wǒ liǎngdiǎn yíkè shàng kè.

帕蘭卡：你幾點下課？
Palanka: Nǐ jǐdiǎn xià kè?

古　波：四點二十下課。
Gubo: Sìdiǎn èrshí xià kè.

帕蘭卡：下課以後你有事兒嗎？
Palanka:　Xià kè yǐhòu nǐ yǒu shìr ma?

古　波：沒有事兒。我回宿舍看書。晚上我跟朋友一起去看
Gubo:　Méi yǒu shìr. Wǒ huí sùshè kàn shū. Wǎnshang wǒ gēn péngyou yìqǐ qù kàn

電影。
dìanyǐng.

帕蘭卡：你看幾點的？
Palanka:　Nǐ kàn jǐdiǎn de?

古　波：我看八點的。你去不去？
Gubo:　Wǒ kàn bādiǎn de. Nǐ qù bu qù?

帕蘭卡：我不去。下課以後，我們去咖啡館，好嗎？
Palanka:　Wǒ bú qù. Xià kè yǐhòu, wǒmen qù kāfēiguǎn, hǎo ma?

古　波：好啊。你四點半在那兒等我。
Gubo:　Hǎo a. Nǐ sìdiǎnbàn zài nàr děng wǒ.

帕蘭卡：我跟丁雲一起去。
Palanka:　Wǒ gēn Dīng Yún yìqǐ qù.

古　波：太好了。你們坐車去嗎？
Gubo:　Tài hǎo le. Nǐmen zuò chē qù ma?

帕蘭卡：不，我們走去。
Palanka:　Bù, wǒmen zǒu qù.

古　波：好，四點半再見。

Gubo:　Hǎo, sìdiǎnbàn zàijiàn.

二、生　詞

1.點	diǎn	a measure word, o'clock
2.食堂	shítáng	dining-hall
3.差	chà	to lack, to be short of
4.分	fēn	a measure word, minute
5.刻	kè	a measure word, quarter (of an hour)
6.上（課）	shàng(kè)	to attend (a class), to teach (in a class)
7.課	kè	class, lesson
8.下（課）	xià(kè)	class is over or dismissed
9.以後	yǐhòu	later on, in the future
10.事兒	shìr	business, thing
11.回	huí	to return, to go back to
12.跟	gēn	with, to follow, to accompany
13.一起	yìqǐ	together
14.電影	diànyǐng	film, movie
15.咖啡館	kāfēiguǎn	café
咖啡	kāfēi	coffee
16.半	bàn	half

(211, 212)

— 154 —

17.啊	a	a modal particle
18.等	děng	to wait
19.走	zǒu	to depart, to walk

補　充　詞

1.上班	shàng bān	to go to work, to start working
2.下班	xià bān	to come or go off work
3.電影院	diànyǐngyuàn	cinema
4.錶	biǎo	watch
5.鐘	zhōng	clock
6.以前	yǐqián	before, in the past, ago

三、閱讀短文

　　Jiākè是古波的好朋友，他也學習漢語，他跟古波在一個班。他們常常一起去看電影。

　　今天(jīntiān, today)有一個新電影，是中國的。Jiākè晚上沒有事兒，他找古波看電影。十二點，他去電影院　買電影票，十二點半他坐車去宿舍找古波，古波不在。

　　古波今天有課，他很忙。一點半他去食堂，兩點一刻還有口語課。帕蘭卡差五分兩點來找他，她告訴古波，下午四點半她跟丁雲一起去咖啡館。古波說：“好，現在我去上課，四點半再見。”

[see page 168]

　　　　　　　　　(212, 217, 218)

四、注釋 Notes

1. "下課以後你有事兒嗎？"

As well as standing alone, the phrase "以後" (or "以前") may be used after a word or phrase denoting time, e.g. "兩點以後", "認識以後", "來中國以後"。

"有事兒" means "to have something to do" or "to be engaged in..."

2. "好啊。"

"啊" here is a modal particle, showing affirmation, approval or consent, and is pronounced in the neutral tone.

3. "我跟丁雲一起去。"

The prepositional construction "跟…", which is made up of the preposition "跟" and its object, is very often used in front of the verb as an adverbial adjunct. Besides, "跟…" frequently goes with the adverb "一起" to form the construction "跟…一起" which means "together with".

4. "你們坐車去嗎？"

"你們坐車去嗎？" is another instance of a sentence with verbal constructions in series. In sentences of this kind, the first verb usually tells the manner of the action expressed by the second verb, as in "走路去", "用筆寫" and "用漢語介紹".

五、替換與擴展　Substitution and Extension

㈠

1. 現在幾點?
   現在兩點。

3：05	6：30
4：15	10：45
5：20	11：58

2. 你幾點上課?
   我兩點一刻上課。

下課,	12：10
去食堂,	12：30
上班*,	8：00
下班*,	4：00
去咖啡館,	4：30

3. 你現在有課嗎?
   有課。
   下課以後你作什麼?
   我回宿舍看書。

去商店買襯衫
回家寫信
去閱覽室看報
去咖啡館喝茶
去電影院*買票

4. 你常常坐車去學院嗎?
   我常常坐車去學院。

來學院　回宿舍
去圖書館　回家

5. 你跟誰一起去?
   我跟我朋友一起去。
   他叫什麼名字?
   他叫 Jiǎkè 。

住
走
工作
學習
看電影

6. 兩點一刻你在哪兒等我？

我在<u>咖啡館</u>等你。

食堂	書店
家	宿舍

(二)

1. Asking the time

A：請問，您的錶* 現在幾點？

B：差五分九點。我的錶* 快 (kuài, fast) 。

你看，那兒是郵局* 的

鐘*，現在八點五十。

A：謝謝。

2. Making an appointment

A：晚上你有事兒嗎？

B：沒有事兒。

A：你來我家，好嗎？

B：好啊。幾點？

A：七點半，好嗎？

3. Making an invitation

A：喂，晚上我們看電影，好嗎？

B：什麼電影？

A：中國電影，是新的。

B：太好了，你買幾點的票？

A：我去買八點十分的票，好嗎？

B：好。七點五十我在家等你，我們一起坐車去。

(215, 216, 217)

— 158 —

* * *

便條 (biàntiáo, note)

> 丁雲：你好！
>
> 　今天下午三點半我来找你，你不在宿舍。我告訴你，明天晚上八點我们學校有一個中文電影，我們一起去看好嗎？你明天晚上七點来我家，我在家等你，再見！
>
> 　　　　　　　帕蘭卡　五月三日

六、語法　Grammar

1. Ways of telling the time

2 : 00	兩點
2 : 05	兩點五分
2 : 12	兩點十二分
2 : 15	兩點一刻（兩點十五分）
2 : 30	兩點半（兩點三十分）
2 : 45	兩點三刻（差一刻三點）
2 : 55	差五分三點（兩點五十五分）
3 : 00	三點

2. Nouns or numeral-measure words denoting time as adverbial adjuncts:

A noun or a numeral-measure word such as "現在", "晚上", "以後"

or " 兩點十分 " can be used as the subject, predicate or attributive of a sentence. E.g.

現在兩點。

今天星期三。 (See p. 155)

他看晚上的電影。

我去買八點十分的票。

Such a noun or numeral-measure word can be used as an adverbial adjunct as well. When so used, it can be put either between the subject and the main element of the predicate or before the subject (in this case special emphasis is laid on the time). E.g.

Nouns or pronouns	Time words	Verbs and other elements
我們	晚上	去看電影。
我	兩點一刻	上課。
你	下課以後	有事兒嗎?
我	三點以前	在家

Time words	Nouns or pronouns	Verbs and other elements
晚上	我們	去看電影。
兩點一刻	我	上課。
下課以後	你	有事兒嗎?
三點以前	我	在家。

Points to be noted:

(1) When used adverbially, a noun or a numeral-measure word denoting time does not necessarily take a preposition before it, and it is wrong to say "我在兩點一刻上課".

(2) Such a noun or numeral-measure word, when used adverbially, can never be put at the end of the sentence. Therefore, you can't say "我們去看電影晚上".

(3) If there is more than one adverbial of time in a sentence, the time word denoting the biggest time unit usually precedes those denoting the smaller time units. That is why "晚上八點我去看電影" is correct and "八點晚上我去看電影" is wrong.

(4) In a sentence, if there are both an adverbial of time and an adverbial of place to simultaneously qualify the verb, the former usually precedes the latter.

Nouns or pronouns	Time words	Position words	Verbs and other elements
你們 我姐姐 他	四點半 現在 晚上	在那兒 在食堂 從咖啡館	等我。 工作。 來我這兒。

Time words	Nouns or pronouns	Position words	Verbs and other elements
四點半 現在 晚上	你們 我姐姐 他	在那兒 在食堂 從咖啡館	等我。 工作。 來我這兒。

3. Tag question " …, 好嗎？ "

The tag question " …, 好嗎？" is often used to make a request or a suggestion and ask for the opinion of the person addressed. The first part of such a tag question is usually a statement. E.g.

晚上你來這兒，好嗎？

我們跟他一起去，好嗎？

下課以後我們去咖啡館，好嗎？

你用英語給我們介紹這個京劇，好嗎？

The usual form of answer to this type of question is " 好啊 " or " 好 ", indicating consent or agreement of the person addressed.

七、練習 Exercises

1. Read out the following phrases and make sentences with them:

   (1) 下課以後　回家以後　來中國以後

   看電影以後　介紹以後　上課以前 *

   回宿舍以前 *

   (2) 跟老師說中文　跟朋友看電影

   跟丁雲一起去圖書館

   跟他們一起學習　跟誰一起工作

2. Say the following time in Chinese:

6:00	3:30
8:22	4:55
9:45	10:35
7:08	11:57

3. Make up questions asking about the underlined parts of the following sentences, using interrogative pronouns:

   (1) 現在<u>十二點二十五分</u>。

   (2) 我<u>五點半</u>回家。

   (3) 晚上他們<u>學習</u>外語。

   (4) 他跟<u>他弟弟</u>一起去看電影。

   (5) 她坐車去<u>王老師</u>家。

   (6) 下課以後他從<u>學院</u>去圖書館。

4. Ask each other questions on the Reading Text.

5. Make a suggestion to a friend of yours:

   Example　去商店

→A：現在你有事兒嗎?

B：沒有事兒。

A：我們一起去商店好嗎?

B：好。幾點去?

A：現在四點二十，四點半去，好嗎?

B：好。

(1) 看京劇

(2) 去圖書館

6. Write a short passage, using the information given.

　7:35　　坐車去學院

　8:00　　上課

11:55　　下課

　2:15　　去閱覽室看雜誌

　4:30　　跟朋友一起去咖啡館

　5:50　　回宿舍

　7:45　　看電影

八、語音語調　Pronunciation and Intonation

1. Word stress (5)

(1) Most words of three or four syllables have a main stress falling on the last syllable. The usual stress pattern of the trisyllables is "medium-weak-strong". E.g.

咖啡館　圖書館　中文系

留學生　閱覽室　實驗室

The usual stress pattern of the four syllables is "medium-weak-medium-strong". E.g.

外語學院　漢語詞典
中國畫報　中文雜誌

(2)　The modal particles "啊", "嗎" and "呢", etc. are never stressed, but pronounced always in the neutral tone. E.g. "好啊！" "你呢？" "你有事兒嗎？"

2.　Exercises

Read aloud the following words and expressions containing the sounds g and k, paying special attention to the pronunciation of these two sounds:

g:　個　哥哥　中國　工作　公司

k:　刻　上課　下課　口語　課文

第十八課

復　習

一、課　文

丁雲的一天

丁雲是英語系的學生。她從北京來這兒學習。英語系有五
Dīng Yún shì Yīngyǔ xì de xuésheng. Tā cóng Běijīng lái zhèr xuéxí. Yīngyǔ xì yǒu wǔge

個中國留學生。他們都在學生宿舍住。
Zhōngguó liúxuéshēng. Tāmen dōu zài xuésheng sùshè zhù.

丁雲每天六點一刻起床。起床以後，她學習英語和法語。
Dīng Yún měi tiān liùdiǎn yīkè qǐ chuáng. Qǐ chuáng yǐhòu, tā xuéxí Yīngyǔ hé Fǎyǔ.

七點半她坐車去學院。每天上午她都有課。他們八點上課，十
Qīdiǎn bàn tā zuò chē qù xuéyuàn. Měi tiān shàngwǔ tā dōu yǒu kè. Tāmen bādiǎn shàng kè, shí-

一點五十分下課。
yīdiǎn wǔshífēn xià kè.

下課以後，丁雲去食堂吃飯。那是學生食堂，她在那兒認
Xià kè yǐhòu, Dīng Yún qù shítáng chī fàn. Nà shì xuésheng shítáng, tā zài nàr rènshi

(229, 230)

識很多朋友。
hěn duō péngyou.

下午丁雲沒有課，她回宿舍休息。三點她去閱覽室看畫報
Xiàwǔ Dīng Yún méi yǒu kè, tā huí sùshè xiūxi.　　Sāndiǎn tā qù yuèlǎnshì kàn huàbào

和雜誌。有時候她去朋友家，跟朋友說英語，有時候她去老師
hé zázhì.　　Yǒu shíhou tā qù péngyou jiā,　gēn péngyou shuō Yīngyǔ, yǒu shíhou tā qù lǎoshī

那兒問問題。朋友們也常常來看她。
nàr wèn wèntí.　　Péngyoumen yě chángcháng lái kàn tā.

晚上丁雲在宿舍學習。有時候她跟朋友們去看電影，有時
Wǎnshang Dīng Yún zài sùshè xuéxí. Yǒu shíhou tā gēn péngyoumen qù kàn diànyǐng, Yǒu shí-

候給爸爸、媽媽和朋友寫信。她十一點睡覺。
hou gěi bàba, māma hé péngyou xiě xìn.　Tā shíyīdiǎn shuì jiào.

二、生　詞

1. 天	tiān	day
2. 每	měi	every, each
3. 起床	qǐ chuáng	to get up
起	qǐ	to get up, to rise
床	chuáng	bed
4. 上午	shàngwǔ	morning
5. 吃	chī	to eat

6. 飯	fàn	meal, cooked rice, food
7. 多	**duō**	many, much, a lot of
8. 下午	xiàwǔ	afternoon
9. 休息	xiūxi	to rest, to take a rest
10. 有時候	yǒu shíhou	sometimes
時候	shíhou	time
11. 問題	wèntí	question, problem
12. 睡覺	shuì jiào	to go to bed, to sleep
13. 朋友們	péngyoumen	friends

專　名

北京	Běijīng	Beijing

丁雲的一天

1. "丁雲每天六點一刻起床。"

When qualified by the demonstrative pronoun "每", a noun usually takes a measure word before it, as in "每個學生" or "每本書". But the noun "天", when preceded by "每", doesn't need a measure word inserted in between, as in "每天".

The word "每" is often accompanied in the predicate of the sentence by a word or phrase denoting quantity or by the adverb "都", as in "每天上午她都有課".

2. "她在那兒認識很多新朋友。"

When used attributively, the adjective "多" or "少" (shǎo, few, little) is usually preceded by such an adverb as "很", Instead of "多朋友" we practically always say "很多（的）朋友". "的" after "很多" may be omitted.

四、看圖會話 **Talk About These Pictures**

1. Getting acquainted with each other

我介紹一下兒， 你叫什麼名字？

這是…… 你是哪國人？

你在哪兒工作？

(232, 233)

2. Talking about your family

這是誰?

他是不是你哥哥?

他作什麼工作?

你家有幾個人?

你有沒有孩子?

你有幾個孩子?

3. Sending regards

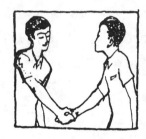

你忙不忙?

問……好

……問你好

4. Talking about the institute

你們學院有幾個系?

你們系有多少學生?

誰教你們語法?

你們下午有課嗎?

5. Asking where someone is going

你從哪兒來?

你去哪兒?

你坐車去嗎?

你跟誰一起去?

6. Talking about an article of clothing

這件襯衫是你的嗎?

哪件襯衫是你的?

你的襯衫是不是綠的?

你的襯衫是新的嗎?

7. Asking the time, and making a suggestion

現在幾點?

你幾點吃飯?

下午你有事兒嗎?

我們去書店, 好嗎?

太好了。

五、語法小結 A Brief Summary of Grammar

1. The subject, predicate, object, attributive and adverbial adjunct

A Chinese sentence is made up of two parts: the subject and the predicate.

The main element of the subject is usually a noun or a pronoun while the main element of the predicate is a verb or an adjective etc. The subject normally precedes the predicate. E.g.

這本書是新的。

丁雲去商店。

你好!

In a conversation, the subject is often omitted. E.g.

你幾點下課?

（我）四點一刻下課。

The predicate can also be omitted if the context or situation leaves no room for misunderstanding. E.g.

你好嗎?

我很好，你呢?

The object, which may be either a noun or a pronoun, forms part of the predicate and usually follows the predicative verb. A number of verbs may have two objects. E.g.

他有一個哥哥。

我認識他。

王老師教我們漢語。

An attributive is mainly used to qualify a noun and is placed before the noun it qualifies. Nouns, pronouns, adjectives, numeral-measure words etc. may all function as attributives.

An adverbial adjunct is mainly used to qualify a verb or an adjective. Adverbs, adjectives, nouns and prepositional constructions etc. may all function as adverbial adjuncts. Adverbial adjuncts regularly precede the words they qualify instead of coming after them. E.g.

我很好。

他們都學習漢語。

上午我們沒有課。

我朋友從北京來。

2. Attributives and the structural particle " 的 " (1)

(1) When used attributively to show possession, a noun usually takes
" 的 " after it. E.g.

媽媽的車

圖書館的書

When a noun is used attributively to indicate the characteristic or
quality of the object denoted by the word it qualifies, it usually doesn't
take " 的 " after it. E.g.

中國人　中國地圖　外語學院

京劇票　學生宿舍　法文電影

英語系　漢語詞典　中文雜誌

(2) When used attributively to show possession, a personal pronoun
usually takes " 的 " after it. E.g.

她的筆　我們的閱覽室

他們的問題

But if the word that the personal pronoun modifies refers to a family
relation or a unit to which the person denoted by the pronoun belongs, the
personal pronoun usually does not take " 的 " after it. E.g.

你哥哥　我家　你們系

(3) When used attributively, a numeral-measure word (or a demonstrative pronoun together with a measure word) usually takes no " 的 " after it.
E.g.

兩張票　九十八個學生　這條裙子

(4) When used attributively a monosyllabic adjective usually takes no
" 的 " after it. E.g.

男朋友　白襯衫　新地圖

(5) An adjective construction, when used attributively, must take "的" after it, e.g. "很好的朋友". The adjective "多" or "少", when used attributively, usually has an adverb before it but doesn't take a "的" after it. e.g. "很多朋友".

六、練習　Exercises

1. Supply each of the following verbs with one or two (direct and indirect) objects, then make a sentence with the verb:

   (1) 等　　說　　寫　　看　　認識
   　　在　　買　　有　　找　　學習
   　　穿　　回　　去　　用　　介紹
   (2) 問　　還　　教　　給　　告訴

2. Answer the following questions:

   (1) 你每天幾點起床？
   (2) 起床以後你作什麼？
   (3) 你每天上午都有課嗎？
   (4) 你每天上午幾點上課？
   (5) 你每天都坐車去學院嗎？
   (6) 你每天都在食堂吃飯嗎？
   (7) 你每天下午都在宿舍嗎？
   (8) 你每天都去圖書館嗎？
   (9) 你常常去咖啡館嗎？
   (10) 每天晚上你都看電影嗎？

⑾ 晚上你常常作什麼?

⑿ 你每天幾點睡覺?

3. Fill in each blank with all the three words or phrases given in brackets in turn, adding the structural particle "的" where necessary:

(1) 這是 ____ 雜誌。(我　中文　閱覽室)

(2) 我有 ____ 朋友。(一個　很多　中國)

(3) 她穿 ____ 裙子嗎? (藍　她姐姐　舊)

(4) 我哥哥下午去買 ____ 票。(四張　京劇　八點鐘)

(5) 我常常看 _____ 書。(語法　新　我們老師)

4. Put in an appropriate measure word in each of the following sentences:

(1) 我哥哥給我一 __ 語法書。

(2) 那 __ 孩子是他姐姐的。

(3) 我朋友不常去這 __ 食堂吃飯。

(4) 這 __ 襯衫不是新的。

(5) 你去哪 __ 銀行?

(6) 每 __ 學生都有詞典嗎?

(7) 那是一 __ 北京地圖。

(8) 我問王老師兩 __ 問題。

(9) 她不穿那 __ 綠裙子。

⑽ 這課有幾 __ 新漢字?

5. Complete the following dialogues with the appropriate phrases from the list given:

對了　好啊　問…好　謝謝你

我們認識一下兒　太好了

(1) A：他給你這本書。

　　 B：＿＿＿＿＿＿＿＿。

(2) A：王先生問你好。

　　 B：＿＿＿＿＿＿＿＿。

(3) A：我們走去，好嗎？

　　 B：＿＿＿＿＿＿＿＿。

(4) A：＿＿＿＿＿＿＿＿。

　　 B：我叫謝明，我是留學生。

(5) A：你是法國人嗎？

　　 B：＿＿＿＿＿＿＿＿。

(6) A：晚上我們去看中國電影，這是兩張票。

　　 B：＿＿＿＿＿＿＿＿。

6. Correct the following erroneous sentences:

(1) 我朋友不學習漢語在北京。

(2) 誰教你語法嗎？

(3) 她從古波來。

(4) 你常常寫他信嗎？

(5) 帕蘭卡學習漢語從丁雲。

(6) 你有幾漢語詞典？

(7) 你認識不認識那大夫？

(8) 她們是很好朋友們。

(9) 我們班有多中國留學生。

(10) 她的車是新。

(11) 在圖書館不有中文雜誌。

⑿ 他每天上課在八點。

⒀ 她常常寫信用中文。

⒁ 我去宿舍和看我朋友。

第 十 九 課

一、課 文

您 要 什 麼

（ 在咖啡館 ）
(Zài kāfēiguǎn)

服務員：您要什麼？

Fúwùyuán:　Nín yào shénme?

帕蘭卡：我要一杯咖啡。

Palanka:　Wǒ yào yìbēi kāfēi.

服務員：小姐，您也要咖啡嗎？

Fúwùyuán:　Xiǎojiě, nín yě yào kāfēi ma?

古　波：中國人喜歡喝茶，是嗎？

Gubo:　Zhōngguó rén xǐhuan hē chá, shì ma?

丁　雲：是啊，有花茶嗎？

Ding Yun:　Shì a, yǒu huāchá ma?

服務員：沒有花茶，有紅茶。您要紅茶還是要咖啡？
Fúwùyuán: Méi yǒu huāchá, yǒu hóngchá. Nín yào hóngchá háishì yào kāfēi?

丁　雲：不，我要一杯橘子水。
Ding Yuan: Bù, wǒ yào yìbēi júzishuǐ.

古　波：我要一瓶啤酒。
Gubo: Wǒ yào yìpíng píjiǔ.

服務員：好，一杯咖啡、一杯橘子水、一瓶啤酒。
Fúwùyuán: Hǎo, yìbēi kāfēi, yìbēi júzishuǐ, yìpíng píjiǔ.

帕蘭卡：聽，這是我們的民歌。你喜歡古典音樂還是喜歡現代
Palanka: Tīng, zhè shì wǒmen de míngē. Nǐ xǐhuan gǔdiǎn yīnyuè háishì xǐhuan xiàndài

　　　　音樂？
　　　　yīnyuè?

丁　雲：我喜歡你們的古典音樂。
Ding Yun: Wǒ xǐhuān nǐmen de gǔdiǎn yīnyuè.

帕蘭卡：我也很喜歡聽中國音樂。以後請你給我們介紹一下兒
Palanka: Wǒ yě hěn xǐhuan tīng Zhōngguó yīnyuè. Yǐhòu qǐng nǐ gěi wǒmen jièshào yíxiar

　　　　中國音樂。
　　　　Zhōngguó yīnyuè.

古　波：帕蘭卡還喜歡唱歌兒。丁雲，你讓她唱一個歌兒。
Gubo: Pàlánkǎ hái xǐhuan chàng gēr. Dīng Yún, nǐ ràng tā chàng yíge gēr.

帕蘭卡：別聽他的。你教我們中國歌兒，好嗎？

Palanka:　　Bié tīng tā de. Nǐ jiāo wǒmen Zhōngguó gēr, hǎo ma?

丁　雲：好啊。晚上八點以後我常常在宿舍，歡迎你們去。

Ding Yun:　Hǎo a. Wǎnshang bādiǎn yǐhòu wǒ chángcháng zài sùshè, huānyíng nǐmen qù.

二、生　詞

1. 要	yào	to want, to be going to, must
2. 服務員	fúwùyuán	waiter, waitress, attendant
3. 杯	bēi	a measure word, cup
4. 小姐	xiǎojiě	miss, young lady
5. 喜歡	xǐhuān	to like, to be fond of
6. 花茶	huāchá	jasmine tea
7. 紅茶	hóngchá	black tea
紅	hóng	red
8. 還是	háishì	or
9. 橘子水	júzishuǐ	orangeade, orange juice
橘子	júzi	orange
水	shuǐ	water
10. 瓶	píng	a measure word, bottle
11. 啤酒	píjiǔ	beer
12. 聽	tīng	to listen

13.民歌	míngē	folk song
14.古典	gǔdiǎn	classical
15.音樂	yīnyuè	music
16.現代	xiàndài	modern
17.唱	chàng	to sing
18.歌兒	gēr	song
19.讓	ràng	to let, to ask
20.別	bié	don't

補 充 詞

1.枝	zhī	a measure word, branch
2.蘋果	píngguǒ	apple
3.香蕉	xiāngjiāo	banana
4.葡萄	pútao	grape
5.唱片	chàngpiàn	phonograph record
6.糖	táng	sugar, sweets, candy
7.綠茶	lǜchá	green tea

三、閱讀短文

聽 中 國 唱 片

古波和帕蘭卡都喜歡中國音樂。晚上八點半，他們去丁雲

　　　　　　(250, 251, 256)

的宿舍聽唱片。丁雲有很多中國唱片，有現代音樂的，也有古典音樂的。

丁雲請他們喝中國茶。她有花茶和綠茶。古波要花茶，帕蘭卡要綠茶。

古波和帕蘭卡都很喜歡那個歌兒，他們問丁雲：“這是一個民歌，對嗎？”丁雲說：“對了，這是一個民歌。”古波問：“這個歌兒叫什麼名字？”丁雲說：“這個歌兒的名字是《茉莉花》(Mòlihuā, Jasmine Flowers)。”

帕蘭卡請丁雲教他們這個歌兒。丁雲說：“好。”

四、注釋 Notes

1.“你要什麼？”

“你要什麼？” is an expression used to ask what someone wants, an expression employed mostly by shop assistants or restaurant waiters.

2.“中國人喜歡喝茶，是嗎？”

“…，是嗎？”（“…，是不是？” or “…，對嗎？”）is a tag question. It is used to ask the person addressed to confirm one's own estimate of which he is not very sure. In answering it, “是啊”（or “對”）is used if the person addressed agrees to him, and “不” is used if the contrary is the case.

3.“有花茶嗎？”

“有…嗎？” is an expression that a customer uses to ask a shop assistant or a restaurant waiter if they have the thing he wishes to buy. The subject is more often than not omitted.

4.“我也很喜歡聽中國音樂。”

A verb or a verb-object construction can function as the object of the predicative verb. The object of the verb “喜歡” may be either a noun or a verb or a verb-object construction.

“聽音樂” means "to appreciate music".

5.“別聽他的。”

"Don't listen to him."

五、替換與擴展 Substitution and Extension

㈠

1.你要什麼？

我要<u>一杯咖啡</u>。

```
兩，啤酒（瓶）
三，紅茶（杯）
四，橘子水（瓶）
一，水（杯）
```

2. 你要多少電影票？
   我要兩張電影票。

```
詞典（本），五
地圖（張），十二
畫報（本），兩
筆（枝），三
```

3. 你要英文報還是
   要中文報？
   我要中文報。
   他也要中文報。

```
上語法課，上口語課
喝茶，    喝咖啡
找古波，  找帕蘭卡
回家，    去咖啡館
買橘子，  買蘋果
```

4. 她喜歡古典音樂還是喜歡現代音樂？
   她喜歡現代音樂，
   有時候她也聽古典
   音樂。

```
用新筆，用舊筆
穿裙子，穿褲子
吃香蕉，吃葡萄
```

(253, 254, 255)

5. 你請誰<u>介紹中國音樂</u>？
   我請我朋友介紹中國音樂。

唱中國歌	看電影
教你漢語	聽現代音樂
吃飯	買唱片˙

6. 他讓你作什麼？
   他讓我<u>唱一個歌</u>。

寫漢字	給他寫信
問問題	還他的雜誌
看語法	在他家吃飯

（二）

1. Buying some apples

   A：您要什麼？

   B：有好蘋果˙嗎？

   A：有。您要多少？

   B：我要兩公斤 (gōngjīn, kilogram)。

   A：還要什麼？

   B：還要一公斤葡萄。

2. Serving a customer

   A：你要咖啡還是要茶？

   B：我要咖啡。

   A：加 (jiā, to add) 糖˙嗎？

   B：不加糖。

3. Making an invitation

A：現在你有事兒嗎？

B：沒有。

A：我們去咖啡館，我請你喝咖啡，好嗎？

B：好啊，謝謝你。

4. Asking someone's opinions about something

A：你喜歡不喜歡
這本書？

B：我不太喜歡。

A：我很喜歡這本
書。

六、語法 Grammar

1. Alternative questions

An alternative question is one formed of two statements joined by "還是" suggesting two different alternatives for the person addressed to choose from. E.g.

你去還是不去？

——我去。

你喜歡古典音樂還是喜歡現代音樂？

——我喜歡現代音樂。

你回家還是去咖啡館？

——我回家。

(255, 256, 257)

他下午去圖書館還是晚上去圖書館？

——他晚上去圖書館。

Here are two forms of how a "是" sentence is turned into an alternative question:

這杯茶是你的還是他的？

——這杯茶是他的。

他是老師還是學生？

——他是學生。

2. Pivotal sentences

In Chinese, there is a kind of sentence with a verbal predicate composed of two verbal constructions in which the object of the first verb is at the same time the subject of the following verb. Such a sentence is known as a pivotal sentence. In a pivotal sentence the first verb is often such a causative verb as "請" or "讓" etc.

Nouns or pronouns	Verbs	Nouns or pronouns	Verbs	Nouns or pronouns
帕蘭卡	請	丁雲	教	中國歌兒。
她	請	我們	去	她家。
老師	讓	他	寫	什麼？
爸爸	不讓	這個孩子	喝	啤酒。

Both "請" and "讓" mean to ask someone to do something. "請" is much more polite and may also be used to mean "to invite", as in "他請我吃飯".

(257, 258, 259)

七、練習 Exercises

1. Read out the following phrases and make sentences with them:

 (1)現代音樂　現代英語　現代語法

 　　現代口語　現代漢語詞典

 (2)喜歡看　喜歡學習　喜歡作

 　　喜歡用　喜歡吃　喜歡喝　喜歡穿

2. Make alternative questions in the same way as the examples given, using the following groups of words, and then answer them:

 Example　橘子水　你的　他的

 　　　　→這杯橘子水是你的還是他的？

 　　　　　這杯橘子水是我的。

 (1)雜誌　圖書館的　閱覽室的

 (2)書　英文的　法文的

 (3)襯衫　新的　舊的

 (4)裙子　紅的　綠的

 Example　去咖啡館　上午　下午

 　　　　→你上午去咖啡館還是下午去咖啡館？

 　　　　　我下午去咖啡館。

 (1)起床　6:15　6:30

 (2)上課　8:00　8:20

 (3)看朋友　下午　晚上

 (4)睡覺　10:30　11:00

 (5)給他寫信　現在　以後

Example 下午　去書店　去商店

　　→他下午去書店還是去商店？

　　他下午去書店。

(1)現在　教漢語　教外語

(2)以後　學習英語　學習法語

(3)下課以後　休息　復習課文　(See p. 245)

(4)每天晚上　在宿舍　在學院

3. Answer the following questions on the Reading Text:

(1)古波和帕蘭卡喜歡不喜歡中國音樂？

(2)他們去哪兒聽中國唱片？

(3)丁雲請他們喝什麼？

(4)他們喜歡喝什麼茶？

(5)古波和帕蘭卡喜歡哪一個歌兒？

(6)那是什麼歌兒？

(7)他們請丁雲作什麼？

4. Make up questions asking about the underlined parts of the following sentences, using suitable interrogative pronouns:

(1)王先生讓他們寫<u>漢字</u>。

(2)帕蘭卡請<u>丁雲</u>教她漢語。

(3)我們請<u>她朋友</u>在北京買兩本語法書。

(4)<u>古波</u>請我去看電影。

(5)我朋友請我去<u>他家</u>吃飯。

5. Make up dialogues in the same way as the following examples, using the information given:

Example 中文雜誌　兩本

→ A: 您要什麼？

B: 我要中文雜誌。

A: 您要幾本？

B: 我要兩本。

(1)啤酒　五瓶

(2)《中國民歌》　一本

(3)七點五十的電影票　兩張

Example　咖啡　紅茶

→ A: 你要咖啡嗎？

B: 謝謝，我不要咖啡。

請（你）給我一杯紅茶。

(1)啤酒　橘子水

(2)紅茶　花茶

(3)中文畫報　英文畫報

八、語音練習　Pronunciation and Intonation

1. Sense group stress (1)

A sense group is a series of syllables that express a comparatively complete idea and can be uttered in one breath. A sense group may be a short sentence or part of a sentence. All sense groups have one of its syllables uttered with greater force than the others: this is known as "sense group stress". Sense group stress is given merely by uttering a stressed syllable with slightly greater force, and it does not shift the position of word stress, making originally unstressed syllables stressed ones. Sense group stress is closely related to sentence structure and can be determined by an analysis of the sentence elements (in this book the sense group stress is marked with the sign " ～～ ").

(1) In Subject + Predicate constructions, the predicate is usually stressed. E.g.

你們認識嗎？

——我們認識。

你去嗎？

——我去。

現在幾點？

——現在兩點半。

The word "是" in "是" sentences is usually not stressed, but the words that follow are stressed. E.g.

她是丁雲。

這是我們的民歌。

(2) In Subject + Verb + Object constructions, the object is stressed.

我要咖啡。

中國人喜歡茶。

丁雲有姐姐，沒有妹妹。

(3) Attributive modifiers are usually stressed. E.g.

你喜歡中國音樂嗎？

這是新裙子，那是舊裙子。

Points to be noted:

(1) Personal pronouns used attributively are usually unstressed, but the the nouns that follow are stressed. E.g.

我喜歡你們的民歌。

(2) Attributive modifiers formed of the numeral " 一 " and a measure word are not stressed. All other numeral-measure words, when used attributively, are usually stressed. E.g.

我要一瓶啤酒。

你要兩杯咖啡。

(3) In attributive modifiers formed of a series of words, the word closest to the head-word is usually stressed. E.g.

他喜歡你們的現代音樂。

帕蘭卡喜歡中國的新民歌。

2. Exercises

Read aloud the following folk rhyme:

Yípiàn   qīng   lai   yípiàn   huáng,
一片　　青　來　一片　　黃，

huáng shì màizi   qīng shì yāng.
黃　是　麥子　青　是　秧

Shì   shéi xiù   chū   huā   shìjiè,
是　誰　繡　出　花　世界，

láodòng   rémín   shǒu   yìshuāng
勞動　　人民　手　一雙。

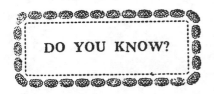

Chinese Tea

In many languages the word for "tea" originated from Chinese, for China is the home of tea shrubs and one of the oldest tea growing and producing countries in the world. China is well-known for her great varieties of tea and their fine quality. Chinese tea falls into different kinds because of the different methods by which tea leaves are processed. There are mainly five kinds: black tea (e.g. Keemun black tea, produced in Qiman County, Anhui Province), green tea (e.g. Lung Jing tea, produced in Hangzhou, Zhejiang Province), scented tea, Oolong tea, white tea and other kinds.

Tea is the favourite drink of the Chinese people. Visitors to a Chinese home are invariably served with tea as well as with candies and cookies. The Chinese usually make their tea by pouring boiling hot water into a tea-pot with tea leaves in it, and putting the lid back on, and the tea is ready for drinking in few minutes' time. Then they pour the tea not into a teacup. Most Chinese prefer green tea or scented tea, usually with no sugar or lemon in it.

(269, 270)

第 二 十 課

一、課 文

四月二十八號是我的生日

（下課以後）
(Xià kè yǐhòu)

古　波：王老師，您今天還有課嗎？
Gubo:　Wáng Lǎoshī, nín jīntiān hái yǒu kè ma?

　王　：有。十點一刻我給他們班上課。今天的語法你們有問
Wang:　Yǒu. Shídiǎn yíkè wǒ gěi tāmen bān shàng kè.　Jīntiān de yǔfǎ nǐmen yǒu wèn-

　　　　題嗎？
　　　　tí ma?

古　波：我有兩個問題。帕蘭卡也有問題。
Gubo:　Wǒ yǒu liǎngge wèntí. Pàlánkǎ yě yǒu wèntí.

　王　：好，下午我來給你們輔導。你們兩點來還是三點來？
Wang:　Hǎo, xiàwǔ wǒ lái gěi nǐmen fǔdǎo.　Nǐmen liǎngdiǎn lái háishì sāndiǎn lái?

帕蘭卡：我們三點來。老師，二十八號晚上您有空兒嗎？
Palanka: Wǒmen sāndiǎn lái. Lǎoshī, èrshibāhào wǎnshang nín yǒu kòngr ma?

王　　：你們有什麼事兒？
Wang: Nǐmen yǒu shénme shìr?

帕蘭卡：四月二十八號是我的生日。我今年二十歲。
Palanka: Sìyuè èrshibāhào shì wǒ de shēngri. Wǒ jīnnián èrshisuì.

王　　：是嗎？祝賀你！
Wang: Shì ma? Zhùhè nǐ!

帕蘭卡：謝謝。我家有一個舞會，請您參加，好嗎？
Palanka: Xièxie. Wǒ jiā yǒu yíge wǔhuì, qǐng nín cānjiā, hǎo ma?

古　波：我們班的同學都參加。
Gubo: Wǒmen bān de tóngxué dōu cānjiā.

王　　：那一定很有意思。今天幾號？
Wang: Nà yídìng hěn yǒu yìsi. Jīntiān jǐ hào?

古　波：今天四月二十六號，星期五。四月二十八號是星期日。
Gubo: Jīntiān sìyuè èrshiliùhào, xīngqīwǔ. Sìyuè èrshibāhào shì xīngqīrì.

王　　：好，我一定去。
Wang: Hǎo, wǒ yídìng qù.

帕蘭卡：太好了。您知道我家的地址嗎？
Palanka: Tài hǎo le. Nín zhīdao wǒ jiā de dìzhǐ ma?

王　　：我知道。

Wang:　Wǒ zhīdao.

二、生　詞

1.月	yuè	month
2.日	rì	date, day of the month
3.生日	shēngri	birthday
4.今天	jīntiān	today
5.班	bān	class
6.輔導	fǔdǎo	to coach
7.號	hào	date, day of the month
8.空兒	kòngr	spare time, free time
9.今年	jīnnián	this year
10.歲	suì	a measure word, year (age)
11.祝賀	zhùhè	to congratulate, congratulation
12.舞會	wǔhuì	dance, ball
13.參加	cānjiā	to take part in, to attend
14.同學	tóngxué	classmate, schoolmate
15.一定	yídìng	surely, certainly, certain, given, particular
16.有意思	yǒu yìsi	interesting, fun
17.星期	xīngqī	week

(274, 275)

18.星期日	xīngqīrì	Sunday
19.知道	zhīdao	to know
20.地址	dìzhǐ	address
21.年	nián	year

補 充 詞

1.去年	qùnián	last year
2.明年	míngnián	next year
3.音樂會	yīnyuèhuì	concert
4.結婚	jié hūn	to get married
5.對不起	duì bu qǐ	(I'm) sorry
6.約會	yuēhuì	appointment, date
7.沒關係	méi guānxi	it doesn't matter
8.談	tán	to talk, to chat

三、閱讀短文

丁雲給爸爸的信

親愛 (qīn'ài, dear) 的爸爸：

您好。

我現在很忙，每天上午都去學院上課。星期一、星期三有語法課，星期二、星期四和星期五有口語課，星期三下午有歷

—197—

史(lìshǐ, history) 課。我還常常去閱覽室看畫報和雜誌。今天是星期四，晚上我有空兒，給您寫信。

這兒的老師和同學們都很好。我現在有很多朋友。帕蘭卡是我的新朋友，她今年二十歲，是外語學院的學生。她爸爸教我們歷史，她媽媽是大夫，他們常常問您好。星期日是帕蘭卡的生日，她家有一個舞會，請我們中國同學參加。

媽媽好嗎？姐姐工作忙不忙？問她們好，我很想你們。

祝您

健康(jiànkāng, health)

雲

1981 年 4 月 25 日

四月二十八號是我的生日

(282)

—198—

四、注釋　Notes

1. "今天的語法你們有問題嗎？"

"Do you have any questions about today's grammar lesson?"

2. "你有空兒嗎？"

"你有空兒嗎？" means "Are you free?" or "Do you have some time to spare?" It is used when one wishes to make an appointment with some-one or ask someone to do something. The negative answer to it is "我没(有) 空兒".

3. "是嗎？祝賀你！"

"是嗎？" here implies that one is surprised to know something he didn't know before. Sometimes it implies disbelief on the part of the speaker.

"祝賀你" is an expression used to offer congratulations.

4. "我們班的同學都參加。"

The word "同學" means "classmate" or "schoolmate", as in "他是我 同學". It is also a form of address for students, e.g. "丁雲同學", "同學們". But it is rare to address "丁雲學生" or "學生們".

5. "那一定很有意思。"

"It must be very interesting."

五、替換與擴展　Substitution and Extension

㈠

1. 今年一九八一年。

| 去年 *，一九八〇 |
| 明年 *，一九八二 |

- 199 -

2. 今天（幾月）幾號?

　今天<u>四月二十五號</u>。

　現在幾點?

　現在<u>三點一刻</u>。

1981 四月小 21 星期二	1981 七月大 1 星期三	1981 十二月大 31 星期四

3. 今天幾號? 星期幾?

　今天<u>十一號</u>，<u>星期四</u>。

　你上午有課還是下午有課?

　我<u>下午</u>有課。

日	一	二	三	四	五	六
	1	2	3	4	5	6
7	8	9	10	11	12	13
14	15	16	17	18	19	20
21	22	23	24	25	26	27
28	29	30	31			

4. 星期二是幾號?
   星期二是八月十五號。

┌─────────────┐
│ 你的生日   │
│ 舞會   │
│ 音樂會*   │
└─────────────┘

5. 你幾號去你朋友家?
   我（六月）二十二號
   去我朋友家。

┌──────────────────┐
│ 去北京　有輔導   │
│ 來　　去聽音樂會 │
│ 休息　有空兒   │
└──────────────────┘

6. 星期日你作什麼?
   星期日我去看同學。
   每個星期日你都去看同學嗎?
   不，有時候我去看電影。

┌─────────────┐
│ 在家寫信   │
│ 看京劇   │
│ 參加舞會   │
│ 在宿舍寫漢字 │
└─────────────┘

7. 他今年二十二歲還是二十三歲?
   他今年二十二歲。

┌──────────────┐
│ 8,　　9   │
│ 32,　33   │
│ 40,　42   │
└──────────────┘

　　　　　　(278, 279)

1. Offering congratulations

    A：我星期六結婚*。

    B：太好了，祝賀你!

    A：謝謝。

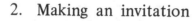

2. Making an invitation

    A：五號下午有空兒嗎?

    B：什麼事兒?

    A：我請你去聽音樂，好嗎? ——是現代音樂。

    B：那一定很有意思。我喜歡聽現代音樂，我一定去。

    *　　　*　　　*

    A：星期四晚上你有空兒嗎?

    B：什麼事兒?

    A：我們去參加舞會，好嗎?

    B：對不起*，星期四晚上我有一個約會*。

    A：沒關係*。

3. Making an appointment

    A：你什麼時候有空兒?

    B：你有事兒嗎?

    A：我跟你談談*，好嗎?

    B：今天晚上七點我在家。

    A：好，我一定去。

    B：這是我家的地址。

    *　　　*　　　*

通知 (tōngzhī, notice)

舞　會

一九八一年十月十五日（星期四）晚上七點半在俱樂部

舉行舞會，歡迎老師和同學們參加。

俱樂部　十月十一日

六、語法　Grammar

1. “年”，“月” and “星期”

In Chinese, the four figures making up the name of a year are read out
as four separate numbers, such as:

一九七九年 (yījiǔqījiǔnián)

一九八〇年 (yījiǔbālíngnián)

一九八五年 (yījiǔbāwǔnián)

In Chinese, the names of the twelve months of the year are:

一月	January	二月	February	三月	March
四月	April	五月	May	六月	June
七月	July	八月	August	九月	September
十月	October	十一月	November	十二月	December

(281, 282, 283)

The names of the seven days of the week are:

星期一 Monday 星期二 Tuesday 星期三 Wednesday
星期四 Thursday 星期五 Friday 星期六 Saturday
星期日（星期天）Sunday

2. The order of the year, month, day and hour

When given simultaneously in a date, the year, month, day and hour are arranged in the following order:

年　月　日（星期　）上（下）午　時

For example:

一九四九年十月一日
一九八一年十月二十六日（星期一）

To refer to a particular day, both "日" and "號" are used. "號" is used mostly in spoken language, and "日" in written language.

Note that in modern Chinese, nouns denoting time such as "年", "月", "日" and "星期" cannot stand all by themselves but must be preceded by a numeral or other words.

3. Sentences with a nominal predicate

A sentence in which the main element of the predicate is a noun, a nominal construction or a numeral-measure word is called a sentence with a nominal predicate. The verb "是" is, as a rule, not used in a sentence of this kind. Such a sentence is mainly used to show time, quantity, one's age or native place etc.

(283, 284)

— 204 —

Nouns or pronouns	Nouns or numeral-measure words
今天	四月二十五號。
現在	幾點?
今天	星期三嗎?
她	今年二十歲,還是二十一歲?
我	北京人。

"不是" is added in front of the predicative noun to make the sentence negative. E.g.

今天不是四月二十五號。

現在不是兩點三十五分。

她今年不是二十歲。

Note that in a sentence of this kind, however, the verb "是" can also be used in front of the main element of the predicate. Thus, it becomes a sentence with a verbal predicate. E.g.

今天是星期日。

星期二是八月十五號。

現在是兩點三十五分嗎?

(285, 286)

七、練習 Exercises

1. Read out the following phrases and make sentences with them:

(1) 我們班　　我們班的同學

他們系　　他們系的老師

你們學院　你們學院的學生

(2) 一年　一個月　一個星期　一天

兩年　兩個月　兩個星期　兩天

每年　每個月　每個星期　每天

2. Answer the following questions:

(1) 一年有幾個月?

(2) 一個星期有幾天?

(3) 這個月有多少天?

(4) 這個月有幾個星期天?

(5) 今天幾月幾號?

(6) 今天星期幾?

(7) 星期天是幾號?

(8) 星期天你常常作什麼?

3. Translate the two passages into English, and then put them orally back into Chinese:

(1) 我哥哥今年三十二歲。今年九月他去中國教英語。現在他是北京外語學院的老師。他每個月都給我寫信，他還常常給我買中文雜誌和中文書。

(2) 他姐姐在書店工作。她每天都回家。她有兩個好朋友。她

常常請她們去看電影、聽音樂。有時候她跟她們一起去參
加舞會。

4. Suppose a classmate of yours wants to make an appointment with you, tell him about your activities of the week and what time you will be free, booking yourself on the following time-table:

	上午	下午	晚上
星期一	語法課 （8：00 — 10：00）		朋友來 （7：30）
星期二	口語課 （8：25 — 10：25）		聽音樂 （8：00）
星期三	口語課 （10：45 — 12：45）	去圖書館 （3：15）	
星期四	歷史課 （8：20 — 10：20）		看電影 （7：50）
星期五	語法課 （9：15 — 11：15）		
星期六 星期日		參加舞會	朋友結婚 * （7：00）

5. Write a letter to a friend of yours, telling him (or her) about your every-day life at the Institute.

八、語音語調　Pronunciation and Intonation

1.　Sense group stress (2)

(1)　In sentences with a nominal predicate, the predicate is stressed. E.g.

今天幾號?

今天星期五。

他二十二歲。

(2)　When a personal pronoun is used as an object, the verb is stressed, the personal pronoun receiving a weak stress only. E.g.

祝賀你!

謝謝您!

(3)　Adverbial adjuncts are usually stressed. E.g.

我一定去。

我們班的同學都參加。

(4)　Pivotal sentence

In Pivotal word + Verb constructions, the verb is stressed. E.g.

請您參加，好嗎?

In Pivotal word + Verb + Object constructions, the object is stressed. E.g.

以後我請你們聽中國音樂。

2. Exercises

Read aloud the following dialogue, paying attention to the pronunciation of j, q, x and sense group stress:

A : 誰啊? 請進!

B : 你今天去學院嗎?

A : 今天星期幾?

B : 今天星期二。

A : 我去學院，你有事兒嗎?

B : 請你告訴王老師，今天我有事兒，不去上課。

A : 好，我一定告訴他。

B : 謝謝你，再見!

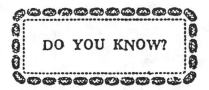

DO YOU KNOW?

China's Lunar Calendar and Main Holidays

China's lunar or Xia calendar, which is said to have come into existence as early as the Xia Dynasty (about 2,100 – 1,600 B.C.), has been in use for several thousand years·and is still in common use today. According to the lunar calendar China's main holidays are as follows:

The Spring Festival This holiday falls on the first day of the first lunar month. It is the most important festival in China, usually celebrated with great pomp, feasting and merry making.

The Clear and Bright Day This holiday falls on the early days of the 3rd, lunar month. On this day people in China visit the graves of their dead to pay them homage.

The Dragon Boat Festival This holiday falls on the 5th day of the 5th lunar month, the traditional day set aside to commemorate Qu Yuan, a great poet and patriot of the ancient Chinese State of Chu.

The Mid-autumn Festival This holiday falls on the 15th day of the 8th lunar month. On the night of this day in China people eat a special kind of pastry called moon-cakes and enjoy looking at the full moon which is particularly clear and bright at the time of the year.

After the founding of the People's Republic of China in 1949, the Gregorian calendar, called the "solar calendar" in China, was adopted. According to the "solar calendar", the main holidays are as follows:

The New Year Day (January 1)

The International Working Women's Day (March 8)

The International Labour Day or May Day (May 1)

The Chinese Youth Day (May 4)

The International Children's Day (June 1)

The Anniversary of the Founding of the Communist Party of China (July 1)

The Army Day (Anniversary of the Founding of the People's Liberation Army) (August 1)

The National Day (October 1)

(294, 295)

第二十一課

一、課 文

這束花兒真好看

（帕蘭卡家。丁雲進。）
(Pàlánkǎ Jiā. Dīng Yún jìn.)

丁　雲：祝你生日好！這是送你的花兒。
Ding Yun:　Zhù nǐ shēngri hǎo! Zhè shì sòng nǐ de huār.

帕蘭卡：啊，這束花兒真好看，非常感謝。今天來的同學很多，
Palanka:　À, zhèshù huār zhēn hǎokàn, fēicháng gǎnxiè. Jīntiān lái de tóngxué hěn duō,

　　　　我真高興。請進。
　　　　wǒ zhēn gāoxìng. Qǐng jìn.

丁　雲：布朗先生、布朗太太，你們好！
Ding Yun:　Bùlǎng Xiānsheng, Bùlǎng Tàitai, nǐmen hǎo!

布　朗：你好。請坐。
Bùlǎng:　Nǐ hǎo. Qǐng zuò.

太　太：丁雲真年輕。你今年多大？
Tàitai:　Dīng Yún zhēn niánqīng. Nǐ jīnnián duō dà?

丁　雲：我今年二十二歲。
Ding Yun:　Wǒ jīnnián èrshièrsuì.

太　太：你的生日是哪一天？
Tàitai:　Nǐ de shēngri shì nǎ yìtiān?

丁　雲：我的生日是二月十六日。
Ding Yun:　Wǒ de shēngri shì èryuè shíliùrì.

帕蘭卡：丁雲，他們都在那兒跳舞。你看，那個年輕的姑娘是
Palanka:　Dīng Yún, tāmen dōu zài nàr tiào wǔ. Nǐ kàn, nàge niánqīng de gūniang shì

　　　　日本人，我給你們介紹介紹。
　　　　Rìběn rén, wǒ gěi nǐmen jièshaojièshao.

丁　雲：好。布朗先生，您坐，我們去看看她。
Ding Yun:　Hǎo. Bùlǎng Xiānsheng, nín zuò, Wǒmen qù kànkan tā.

布　朗：請吧。
Bùlǎng:　Qǐng ba.

太　太：這個中國姑娘很漂亮。
Tàitai:　Zhège Zhōngguó gūniang hěn piàoliang.

布　朗：我說帕蘭卡更漂亮。
Bùlǎng:　Wǒ shuō Pàlánkǎ gèng piàoliang.

太　太：是嗎？
Tàitai:　Shì ma?

布　朗：她像她媽媽。
Bùlǎng:　Tā xiàng tā māma.

*　　　*　　　*

太　太：誰啊？我去開門。啊，是王老師，請進。
Tàitai: Shéi a? Wǒ qù kāi mén.　　À, shì Wáng Lǎoshī, qǐng jìn.

二、生　詞

1.束	shù	a measure word, bunch
2.花兒	huār	flower
3.真	zhēn	real, true, genuine
4.好看	hǎokàn	good-looking
5.祝	zhù	to wish
6.送	sòng	to give as a present, to send
7.非常	fēicháng	extremely, unusually
8.感謝	gǎnxiè	to thank
9.高興	gāoxìng	glad, happy, delighted
10.太太	tàitai	Mrs., madame
11.年輕	niánqīng	young
12.多	duō	how
13.跳舞	tiào wǔ	to dance

14.姑娘	gūniang	girl
15.吧	ba	a modal particle
16.漂亮	piàoliang	pretty, beautiful
17.更	gèng	even, still
18.像	xiàng	to be like, to resemble, to take after
19.開	kāi	to open
20.門	mén	door

專　名

| 1.布朗 | Bùlǎng | a personal name |
| 2.日本 | Rìběn | Japan |

補　充　詞

1.輛	liàng	measure word (for cars)
2.乾淨	gānjing	clean, neat
3.新年	xīnnián	New Year
4.歲數	suìshu	age
5.禮物	lǐwù	present, gift
6.照片	zhàopiàn	photograph, picture
7.兒子	érzi	son
8.女兒	nǚ'ér	daughter

(300, 301)

三、閱讀短文

一 張 照 片

星期天，我們去王老師那兒。他讓我們看他一家人的照片。

王老師是北京語言 (yǔyán, language) 學院的老師，他敎留學生漢語。他常常在國外(guówài, abroad) 工作。王老師今年四十五歲，他愛人今年四十二歲。王老師的愛人在北京圖書館工作。

王老師的兒子叫王中。他很年輕，今年十八歲，是北京大學 (dàxué, university) 的學生。他的學習很好。穿裙子的姑娘是他們的女兒——王英。她今年十歲。王英真漂亮，穿一件白襯衫，紅裙子。她很像她媽媽，她媽媽也非常喜歡她。

五月三號是王英的生日。今天，王老師去商店給女兒買禮物。

(308, 309)

1. "祝你生日好！"

" 祝你…" is used to extend one's good wishes to the person addressed or to offer congratulations in advance. " 祝賀你 ", on the other hand, is used to offer congratulations for something already known or accomplished.

2. "布朗太太"

Forms of address such as " 太太", " 夫人", " 小姐 " and " 女士 " are now used mostly in Taiwan Province, Xianggang (Hong Kong), Aomen (Macao) and in Chinese communities overseas. On China's mainland, however, these forms are not used except on diplomatic occasions. The common form of address on the mainland is now " 同志 " (tóngzhì, comrade).

3. "你今年多大？"

"How old are you?"

In Chinese, in asking about one's age, we can use " 你今年多大" for adults or those who belong to the same generation as oneself; " 你今年幾歲" for children and " 您今年多大歲數(suishu, age)" for the aged or people older than oneself to show politeness or courtesy.

4. "請吧。"

When used at the end of a sentence expressing request, advice, command, consultation or consent or agreement, the modal particle " 吧" (1) softens the tone of the sentence, e.g. " 坐吧！" "休息一下兒吧？" "好吧".

5. "布朗先生，您坐。我們去看看她。"

" 您（你）坐 " or " 您（你）忙吧 " is a polite form used when one wishes to discontinue a conversation or to disengage oneself from some occupation.

6. "我說帕蘭卡更漂亮。"

" 更" is an adverb of degree, often used before an adjective or a verb as an adverbial adjunct to imply, in a number of persons or things of the same category, one particular person or thing possesses a higher degree of the quality indicated.

(301, 302, 303)

五、替換與擴展　　Substitution and Extension

㈠

1. 這束花兒好看嗎?
   這束花兒真好看。
   這束花兒是你的嗎?
   這束花兒是我的。

襯衫	（件）
裙子	（條）
車	（輛）*
照片*	（張）

2. 他們的食堂大不大?
   他們的食堂不太大。

中文書，	多
地圖，	新
老師，	忙
同學，	年輕
孩子，	漂亮
宿舍，	乾淨*

3. 這本畫報好嗎?
   很好。
   那本畫報更好，你看看。

啤酒	（瓶），	喝
歌兒	（個），	唱
詞典	（本），	用
唱片*	（張），	聽
大衣*	（件），	穿

4. 那條漂亮的裙子是誰的?
   是這個姑娘的。

好看，	筆	（枝）*
乾淨*，	襯衫	（件）
漂亮，	本子*	（個）

5. 星期三有沒有課?
   有課。
   來的同學多嗎?
   來的同學很多。

舞會，	參加舞會的人
電影，	看電影的人
音樂會*，	聽音樂會的人
輔導，	參加輔導的同學

6. 你今年多大?
   我今年二十二歲。
   你的生日是哪一天?
   我的生日是五月八日。

19，	2月12日
32，	12月27日
23，	9月29日

7. 祝你生日好!
   謝謝你。

工作	新年*
學習	

1. Asking the age

    A：你爸爸好嗎?

    B：謝謝你，他很好。

    A：他今年多大歲數*?

    B：他今年六十二。

          *   *   *

    A：你有孩子嗎?

    B：我有一個男孩子。

    A：他今年幾歲?

    B：他今年八歲。

          *   *   *

    A：你今年多大?

    B：二十八。

    A：你很年輕，像二十四歲。

    B：是嗎?

2. Asking for opinions from others

    A：這個電影有沒有意思?

    B：很有意思。

    A：以後我也去看看。

3. Presenting a gift

    A：這是給你的禮物*。

    B：啊，你太客氣了!

    A：你喜歡嗎?

    B：我非常喜歡。謝謝你。

賀年片
(hèniánpiàn, New Year's Card)

六、語法　Grammar

1.　Sentences with an adjectival predicate

A sentence in which the main element of the predicate is an adjective is known as a sentence with an adjectival predicate.　In such a sentence the verb "是" is not normally used in the predicate.　E.g.

她今天非常高興。

我的襯衫太大。

這個閱覽室很小。

那個服務員很年輕。

In affirmative sentences of this type, if the simple predicative adjective is not preceded by an adverb of degree such as "真", "太", "非常" or "更", it is usually qualified by the adverb "很".　Without adverbial modifiers of any kind, the adjective often implies comparison, as in:

這個閱覽室小，那個閱覽室大。

那個服務員年輕，這個服務員不年輕。

Points to be noted:

(1)　When used in sentences of this type, "很" does not indicate degree

(308, 309, 310)

as it does elsewhere. "他很忙" and "他忙" have practically the same meaning.

(2) But "很" is not used in the affirmative-negative form of sentence of this type and it is incorrect to say "他很高興不很高興？"

2. Reduplication of verbs

Verbs denoting actions can be repeated or reduplicated. This device is usually employed when one wishes to indicate that the action is of very short duration, to soften the tone of a sentence or to make it sound relaxed or informal. Sometimes a verb is reduplicated to imply that what is done is just for the purpose of trying something out. In the case of dissyllabic verbs, the reduplication follows the pattern "ABAB". E.g.

老師讓我們想想這個問題。

這本畫報很好，你看看。

我們去咖啡館坐坐吧。

請你介紹介紹中國的民歌。

Points to be noted:

(1) Verbs such as "有", "在", "是" and "像" which do not show actions can never be reduplicated.

(2) Generally a reduplicated verb can function neither as an attributive nor as an adverbial adjunct.

3. Verbs, verbal constructions or dissyllabic adjectives as attributives

When used attributively, a verb or a verbal construction must take after it the structural particle "的". So must a dissyllabic adjective. E.g.

今天來的同學很多。

這是給她的電影票。

跟他跳舞的姑娘是法國留學生。

(310, 311, 312)

教你們口語的老師叫什麼名字。

這件漂亮的襯衫是誰的?

七、練習 Exercises

1. Read out the following phrases:

    年輕的大夫　年輕的服務員

    年輕的老師　年輕的同學

    漂亮的車　漂亮的咖啡館

    漂亮的裙子　漂亮的姑娘

    好看的裙子　好看的花兒　好看的筆

    有意思的書　有意思的雜誌

    有意思的電影

2. Answer the following questions (first in the affirmative and then in the negative):

    (1) 你們學院大不大?

    (2) 今天帕蘭卡高興不高興?

    (3) 你現在忙不忙?

    (4) 你的中國朋友多不多?

    (5) 你的車新不新?

    (6) 這個漢字對不對?

    (7) 這件襯衫舊不舊?

3. Change the following to alternative questions:

    (1) 他寫的漢字很對。

    (2) 這個電影沒有意思。

(3) 咖啡館的服務員很年輕。

(4) 那個書店不太大。

(5) 他的筆很好看。

(6) 中國的茶真好。

(7) 他們不太高興。

4. Fill in the blanks with the reduplicated forms of the verbs given:

找　幫助　介紹　用　休息　問

(1) 他請我 ＿＿＿＿＿＿北京。

(2) 我 ＿＿＿＿＿＿ 你的車，好嗎?

(3) 我回家 ＿＿＿＿＿＿ 那本書，星期一給你。

(4) 下課以後你回宿舍 ＿＿＿＿＿＿ 吧。

(5) 我不認識這個漢字，我去學院 ＿＿＿＿＿＿老師。

(6) 我朋友的漢語很好，我請他 ＿＿＿＿＿＿我。

5. Talk with your classmates about your family.

八、語音練習　Pronunciation and Intonation

1. Sense group stress (3)

(1) In sentences with an adjectival predicate, the predicate is stressed. E.g.

這束花兒真好看。

丁雲很年輕。

Note that in sentences of this type, "很" is usually pronounced with a weak stress.

(2) The demonstrative pronoun "這" or "那", when used as a subject

　　　　(313, 314, 315)

or an attributive modifier, is usually stressed. E.g.

這是送你的花兒。

那都是舊的。

那個姑娘是日本人。

2. Word stress (5)

When a monosyllabic verb is reduplicated, the main stress falls on the first syllable, and the syllable that follows is pronounced in the neutral tone. E.g.

看看　說說　聽聽　想想

穿穿　找找　問問　用用

When a dissyllabic verb is reduplicated, the main stress falls on the first and the third syllables, the other two syllables are pronounced in the neutral tone. E.g.

輔導輔導　幫助幫助

休息休息　介紹介紹

3. Exercises

Read out the following dissyllabic words, paying attention to the 2nd tone and word stress.

民歌　房間　年輕　結婚

同學　紅茶　食堂　銀行

詞典　蘋果　啤酒

(315, 316, 317)

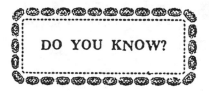

雜誌　郵票　學院

裙子　朋友　時候

Read the following proverb:

Zhǐyào　gōngfu　shēn,

只要　　功夫　　深，

tiěchǔ　　móchéng　zhēn.

鐵杵　　磨成　　針。

(Constant grinding can turn an iron rod into a needle; Perseverance spells success.)

╔══════════════════╗
║ **DO YOU KNOW?** ║
╚══════════════════╝

The Four Treasures for the Study

The writing brush, inkstick, paper and inkslab have been traditionally regarded in China as "the four treasures for a study". They have now had a history of more than 2,000 years. Paper was one of the four great inventions of ancient China. Cai Lun, who lived in the Eastern Han Dynasty (A.D. 25—200), improved the method of papermaking and produced paper of much better quality than before.

Of all the "four treasures for a study", Hu brush (produced originally in Huzhou, now the city of Wuxing, Zhejiang Province), Hui inkstick (produced in the city of Huizhou, Anhui Province), Xuan paper (originally made in the city of Xuancheng, Anhui Province) and Duan inkslab (made from stone quarried in Duanxi area, Gaoyao County, Guangdong Province) are well-known for their high quality to the whole country as top-grade writing materials which are indispensable for traditional Chinese calligraphy and painting.

(317, 319, 320)

第二十二課

一、課　文

後　邊　有　一　個　小　花　園

太　太：請丁雲看看我們的新房子吧。
Taitai:　　Qǐng Dīng Yún kànkan wǒmen de xīn fángzi ba.

帕蘭卡：好。丁雲，跟我來。這是客廳。
Palanka:　Hǎo. Dīng Yún, gēn wǒ lái. Zhè shì kètīng.

丁　雲：這個客廳很大，也很漂亮。
Ding Yun:　Zhège kètīng hěn dà, yě hěn piàoliang.

太　太：客廳旁邊是書房。請進。
Taitai:　　Kètīng pángbian shì shūfáng. Qǐng jìn.

帕蘭卡：這兒有椅子，坐吧。
Palanka:　Zhèr yǒu yǐzi, zuò ba.

丁　雲：謝謝。你們的書真不少。
Ding Yun:　Xièxie. Nǐmen de shū zhēn bù shǎo.

(321, 322)　　　　　　　　　— 226 —

帕蘭卡：桌子上邊的書都是爸爸的。他總不讓我們整理。
Palanka:　Zhuōzi shàngbian de shū dōu shì bàba de. Tā zǒng bú ràng wǒmen zhěnglǐ.

太　太：去看看我們的厨房吧。厨房在對面，從這兒走。
Taitai:　Qù kànkan wǒmen de chúfáng ba. Chúfáng zài duìmiàn, cóng zhèr zǒu.

帕蘭卡：丁雲，我們的厨房太小。
Palanka:　Dīng Yún, wǒmen de chúfáng tài xiǎo.

太　太：不小——作飯的總是我一個人。
Taitai:　Bù xiǎo――zuò fàn de zǒngshì wǒ yíge rén.

帕蘭卡：好了，媽媽，以後我一定幫助你作飯。
Palanka:　Hǎo le, māma, yǐhòu wǒ yídìng bāngzhu nǐ zuò fàn.

太　太：謝謝你。餐廳在厨房左邊，裏邊的房間是我們的臥室。
Taitai:　Xièxie nǐ. Cāntīng zài chúfáng zuǒbian, lǐbian de fángjiān shì wǒmen de wòshì.

帕蘭卡：後邊還有一個小花園。
Palanka:　Hòubian hái yǒu yíge xiǎo huāyuán.

丁　雲：帕蘭卡，你的臥室在哪兒？
Ding Yun:　Pàlánkǎ, nǐ de wòshì zài nǎr?

帕蘭卡：我的臥室在客廳左邊。那是洗澡間。我們的新房子怎
Palanka:　Wǒ de wòshì zài kètīng zuǒbian. Nà shì xǐzǎojiān. Wǒmen de xīn fángzi zěn-

　　　　麼樣？
　　　　meyàng?

丁　雲：你們的新房子非常好。
Ding Yun:　Nǐmen de xīn fángzi fēicháng hǎo.

二、生　詞

1. 後邊	hòubiān	back, at the back of, behind
2. 小	xiǎo	little, small
3. 花園	huāyuán	garden
4. 房子	fángzi	house
5. 客廳	kètīng	drawing room, living room
6. 旁邊	pángbiān	side
7. 書房	shūfáng	study
8. 椅子	yǐzi	chair
9. 少	shǎo	few, little
10. 桌子	zhuōzi	table, desk
11. 上邊	shàngbiān	top, on, over, above
12. 總是	zǒngshì	always
總	zǒng	always
13. 整理	zhěnglǐ	to put in order, to straighten up, to arrange
14. 厨房	chúfáng	kitchen
15. 對面	duìmiàn	opposite
16. 幫助	bāngzhu	to help
幫	bāng	to help

(323, 324, 325)

17.餐廳	cāntīng	dining-hall
18.左邊	zuǒbiān	left
19.裏邊*	lǐbiān	inside
20.房間	fángjiān	room
21.臥室	wòshì	bedroom
22.洗澡間	xǐzǎojiān	bath-room
洗澡	xǐ zǎo	to take a bath
23.怎麼樣	zěnmeyàng	how, how is it that...?

補　充　詞

1.外邊	wàibiān	outside
2.下邊	xiàbiān	bottom, below, under
3.前邊	qiánbiān	front, in front of, before
4.右邊	yòubiān	right
5.中間	zhōngjiān	middle
6.窗戶	chuānghu	window
7.套	tào	a measure word
8.把	bǎ	a measure word

* is interchangeable with 裡

三、閱讀短文

古 波 的 宿 舍

學生城 (Xuéshéngchéng, students' town or university town) 裏邊有很多宿舍，我們認識的古波和中國留學生丁雲也都在那兒住。現在我們去看看古波的宿舍。

古波的宿舍在四層二十九號。他跟他同學一起住。這個房間不太大。門對面是一個很大的窗戶，窗戶旁邊有兩張床：左邊的床是他的，右邊的是他同學的。他們的桌子在兩張床中間。桌子後邊有兩把椅子。房間裏邊有很多漂亮的照片。

古波說："我們的房間不太乾淨 (gānjìng, clean)。現在我們很忙，每天起床以後去學院上課，有時候在圖書館看書。晚上常常十一點回宿舍睡覺。"古波的同學說："古波常常星期五上午整理房間，那天我們的宿舍總是很乾淨——每個星期五下午帕蘭卡都來這兒。"

四、注釋 Notes

1. "（請）跟我來。"

   "(Please) come along with me." or "Come with me, (please)."

   "從這兒走"

   "Come this way."

Both are everyday expressions used to lead the way for someone.

2. "作飯的總是我一個人。"

   "It is always me alone that does the cooking."

"作飯的" means the same as "作飯的人". "的" constructions of this kind, composed of a verb and its object plus "的", are also nominal constructions. Here are some more examples: "吃飯的" (吃飯的人), "學漢語的" (學漢語的人).

3. "好了，媽媽，以後我幫助你作飯。"

"好了" in "好了，媽媽，以後我幫助你作飯。" is used to express the wish to discontinue an argument, meaning "OK, Mama, (you) don't complain anymore. I'll help you with the cooking".

五、替換與擴展　Substitution and Extension

(一)

1. 餐廳在<u>左邊</u>嗎？

   餐廳不在<u>左邊</u>，在<u>右邊</u>。

旁邊，	對面
對面，	後邊
裏邊，	外邊*
上邊，	下邊*

— 231 —

(326, 327)

2. 閱覽室在哪兒?
   閱覽室在<u>圖書館裏邊</u>。
   看書的人多不多?
   看書的人很多。

學校裏邊	
食堂後邊	
實驗室＊對面	
宿舍和食堂中間＊	

3. <u>後邊</u>有什麼?
   後邊有一個<u>花園</u>。
   這個花園大不大?
   這個花園不大。

旁邊，	書房
左邊，	厨房
對面，	洗澡間
前邊＊，	客廳
右邊＊，	臥室

4. <u>食堂裏邊</u>有什麼?
   食堂裏邊有<u>很多桌子和椅子</u>。

圖書館裏邊，	很多書和雜誌
桌子上邊，	兩瓶啤酒
學院旁邊，	一個咖啡館
學院外邊＊，	一個銀行

5. 桌子後邊是什麼?
   桌子後邊是椅子。

書上邊,	筆
桌子上邊,	一束花兒
書下邊*,	兩本畫報
臥室中間*,	一張床
門旁邊,	窗戶

6. 裏邊的房間是誰的?
   裏邊的房間是我們的。

對面的房子,	白先生的
上邊的襯衫,	弟弟的
桌子上邊的信,	你的

7. 你們的新房子怎麼樣?
   我們的新房子很小。

那個咖啡館,	很漂亮
她的裙子,	不好看
今天的電影,	很有意思
這個新餐廳,	不大
這套*房子,	很舊

㈡

1. Asking the way

   A：請問，新郵局*在哪兒?

   B：對不起*，我不知道。

(329, 330)

＊　　＊　　＊

A：請問，這兒有一個新郵局＊嗎？

C：有，在對面，咖啡館旁邊。

A：謝謝你。

C：不謝。

2. On a bus

A：請問，這兒有人嗎？

B：沒有人，坐吧。

A：謝謝。

3. Asking for opinions from others

A：你知道《紅樓夢》(《Hónglóumèng》, "The Dream of the Red Chamber") 嗎？

B：我知道，我有一套＊英文的。

A：這本書怎麼樣？

B：這本書非常好。

＊　　＊　　＊

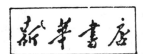 

六、語法　Grammar

1. Position words

Position words are nouns that denote positions and the most commonly used ones are "前邊", "後邊", "上邊", "下邊", "左邊", "右邊", "裏邊",

"外邊", "中間" and "對面". Like ordinary nouns, they may serve as the subject of a sentence, as an object, an attributive and be qualified by an attributive. E.g.

裏邊有什麽?

洗澡間在對面。

桌子上邊有一束花兒。

下邊的報是今天的，你看吧。

左邊的綠車是我的。

Points to be noted:

(1)　When used attributively, a position word usually takes "的" after it, as in "裏邊的房間(the inner room)". But "的" is not used when the position word is itself preceded by an attributive, as in "房間裏邊(inside the room)".

(2)　"裏邊" is not used after geographical names, as in "他在北京學習漢語".

When the preposition "在" is followed by a noun representing a building, an organization or a place, the position word "裏邊" is often omitted, as in "我姐姐在銀行工作", "他在閱覽室看書".

2.　Sentences indicating existence

(1)　"在" indicating existence

The verb "在" very often indicates existence, telling that someone or something is in a certain place. In a sentence with "在", the subject is usually the person or thing concerned and the object is usually a noun denoting position or place.

Nouns or pronouns (persons or things that exist)	Verbs "在"	Nouns or pronouns (positions or locations)
他	在	我左邊。
圖書館	不在	書店旁邊。
我的書	在	你那兒嗎？

(2) "有" indicating existence

Apart from denoting possession, the verb "有" can also indicate existence. In a sentence with "有" as the main element of the predicate, the suject is usually a noun denoting position or place and the object is the person or thing concerned.

Nouns or pronouns (positions or locations)	Verbs "有"	Nouns (persons or things that exist)
後邊	有	一個商店。
這兒	沒有	人。
那本書裏邊	有沒有	照片？

(3) "是" indicating existence

The verb "是" can indicate existence as well. The word order of a "是" sentence, when indicating existence, is exactly the same as that of a "有" sentence.

Nouns or pronouns (positions or locations)	Verbs "是"	Nouns or pronouns (persons or things that exist)
圖書館對面 客廳旁邊 你前邊	是 不是 是	我們學院。 書房。 誰?

Note that there are two points of difference between "是" and "有" when both indicate existence:

(1) Sentences with "有" merely tell where something is located whereas sentences with "是" tell what something is whose whereabouts is already known.

(2) The object of a sentence with "有" is usually indefinite while the object of a sentence with "是" may be either definite or indefinite. So the Chinese for "Our college stands opposite to the library." should be "圖書館對面是我們學院" or "我們學院在圖書館對面" instead of "圖書館對面有我們學院".

七、練習 Exercises

1. Read out the following phrases:

臥室後邊　　後邊的臥室

咖啡館對面　　對面的咖啡館

銀行旁邊　　旁邊的銀行

餐廳左邊　　左邊的餐廳

桌子上邊　　上邊的桌子

新房子　　新地圖　　大花園

舊房子　　舊地圖　　小花園

大房間　　很多老師

小房間　　不少學生

2. Rewrite the following sentences using "有" or "是":

(1) 那杯茶在桌子上邊。

(2) 銀行在書店和咖啡館中間。

(3) 餐廳在廚房外邊。

(4) 花園在房子前邊。

(5) 圖書館在學院左邊。

(6) 客廳在書房旁邊。

3. Fill in the blanks with position words according to the following layout:

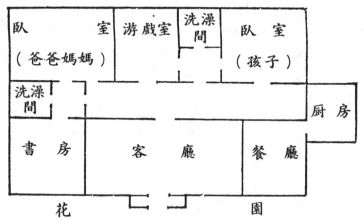

　　這是我家。我家＿＿＿＿有一個花園，花園＿＿＿＿有很多好看的花兒。客廳在房子＿＿＿＿，客廳＿＿＿＿是餐廳。廚房在餐廳＿＿＿＿。客廳＿＿＿＿是爸爸的書房，＿＿＿＿有兩個臥室：

＿＿＿＿的臥室大，是爸爸和媽媽的，＿＿＿＿的臥室小，是我和弟弟的。兩個臥室＿＿＿是我們的遊戲室(yóuxìshì, recreation room)

4. Ask each other questions about the location of the various places identical in the diagram:

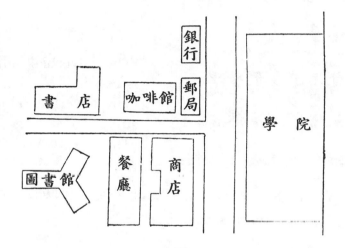

5. Write a short passage as shown by the following picture:

6. Guess what this is:

上邊毛 (máo, hair), 下邊毛，

中間一個水葡萄 (shǔǐ pútáo, watery grape)。

八、語音語調　Pronunciation and Intonation

1. Sense group stress (4)

(1) Adverbial adjuncts are usually stressed. When a negative adverb is used adverbially but the idea of negative is not emphasized, the adverb is usually not stressed. When a verb is followed by an object, the adverbial adjunct, if there is one, is not stressed. E.g.

他常常來。

他不讓我們整理。　(The adverbial adjunct "不" is not stressed.)

裏邊常常有舞會。　(The adverbial adjunct "常常" is not stressed.)

我們晚上去看京劇。　(The adverbial adjunct "晚上" is not stressed.)

(2) When the verbs "有" and "是" indicate existence, they are pronounced with a weak stress. E.g.

後邊有一個小花園。

這是客廳。

裏邊的房間是我們的臥室。

2. Exercises

Read out the following dissyllabic words, paying special attention to the aspirated and unaspirated sounds:

b: 北京　幫助　左邊　本子　上班

p: 旁邊　啤酒　葡萄　蘋果　漂亮

d: 多少　點心　地圖　地址　大夫

t: 聽課　圖書　同學　跳舞　太太

g: 公司　告訴　工作　姑娘　感謝

k: 口語　咖啡　客廳　客氣　好看

Read out the following proverb:

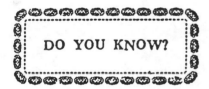

Lù　yáo　zhī　mǎ　lì,
路　遙　知　馬　力，
rì　jiǔ　jiàn　rén　xīn.
日　久　見　人　心。

(As distance tests a horse's strength, so time reveals a person's heart.)

China's Well-known Classical Novels

Most of China's classical novels were produced in the Ming and Qing Dynasties dated from the 14th to 18th centuries. The best-known are "The Romance of the Three Kingdoms" by Luo Guanzhong and "Water Margin" by Shi Naian, both produced in the 14th century, "Pilgrimage to the West" by Wu Chengen and "Jin Ping Mei" by Xiao Xiao Sheng of Langling, both produced in the 16th century, and "The Scholars" by Wu Jingzhi, produced in the 18th century.

(341, 345)

"The Dream of the Red Chamber" written by Cao Xueqin, a great realistic writer of the 18th century, marks the height of China's classical fiction. It occupies an outstanding place in the history of both China's and the world's literature.

第二十三課

一、課 文

我正在看電視呢

帕蘭卡：喂，是學生宿舍嗎？
Palanka: Wèi, shì xuésheng sùshè ma?

工　人：是啊。您找誰？
Gōngrén: Shì a. Nín zhǎo shéi?

帕蘭卡：我找丁雲，請她接電話。
Palanka: Wǒ zhǎo Dīng Yún, qǐng tā jiē diànhuà.

工　人：好，請等一等。
Gōngrén: Hǎo, qǐng děngyideng.

丁　雲：喂，我是丁雲。你是帕蘭卡吧？
Ding Yun: Wèi, wǒ shì Dīng Yún. Nǐ shì Palánkǎ ba?

帕蘭卡：對了，你在休息嗎？
Palanka: Duì le, nǐ zài xiūxi ma?

丁　雲：沒有，我在復習課文呢，你呢？

Ding Yun: Méiyou, wǒ zài fùxí kèwén ne, nǐ ne?

帕蘭卡：我在家裏。我正在看電視呢。

Palanka:　Wǒ zài jiāli. Wǒ zhèngzài kàn diànshì ne.

丁　雲：有什麼新聞？

Ding Yun: Yǒu shénme xīnwén?

帕蘭卡：中國友好代表團正在參觀一個工廠，工人們正歡迎他

Palanka:　Zhōngguó yǒuhǎo dàibiǎotuán zhèngzài cānguān yíge gōngchǎng, gōngrénmen zhèng

　　　　們呢。

　　　　huānyíng tāmen ne.

丁　雲：你們的代表團也在中國訪問呢，報上有他們的照片。

Ding Yun: Nǐmen de dàibiǎotuán yě zài Zhōngguó fǎngwèn ne, bàoshang yǒu tāmen de zhàopiàn.

　　　　古波呢？他怎麼樣？

　　　　Gǔbō ne? Tā zěnmeyàng?

帕蘭卡：他不在，他總是很忙。下午我給他打電話的時候，他

Palanka:　Tā bú zài, tā zǒngshì hěn máng. Xiàwǔ wǒ gěi tā dǎ diànhuà de shíhou, tā

　　　　正上課呢。喂，我説，明天你有空兒嗎？

　　　　zhèng shàng kè ne. Wèi, wǒ shuō, míngtiān nǐ yǒu kòngr ma?

丁　雲：什麼事兒？

Ding Yun:　Shénme shìr?

帕蘭卡：我們去城外玩兒玩兒，好嗎？

Palanka: Wǒmen qù chéngwài wánrwanr, hǎo ma?

丁　雲：好啊。明天幾點出發？

Ding Yun: Hǎo a. Míngtiān jǐdiǎn chūfā?

帕蘭卡：七點半我們開車來接你。

Palanka: Qīdiǎnbàn wǒmen kāi chē lái jiē nǐ.

丁　雲：好，再見！

Ding Yun: Hǎo, zàijiàn!

二、生　詞

1. 正在	zhèngzài	an adverb indicating an action in progress
2. 電視	diànshì	television, TV
3. 接（電話）	jiē (diànhuà)	to answer (the phone)
4. 電話	diànhuà	telephone call, telephone
5. 沒（有）	méi (you)	not, no
6. 復習	fùxí	to review
7. 課文	kèwén	text
8. 新聞	xīnwén	news
9. 友好	yǒuhǎo	friendly
10. 代表團	dàibiǎotuán	delegation
代表	dàibiǎo	delegate, representative
11. 參觀	cānguān	to visit, to pay a visit

12.工廠	gōngchǎng	factory
13.工人	gōngrén	worker
14.訪問	fǎngwèn	to visit, to call on
15.照片	zhàopiàn	photograph, photo, picture
16.打（電話）	dǎ (diànhuà)	to make (a telephone call)
17.明天	míngtiān	tomorrow
18.城	chéng	city, town
19.外邊	wàibiān	outside
20.玩兒	wánr	to play, to have fun with
21.出發	chūfā	to start out, to set off
22.開（車）	kāi (chē)	to drive (a car)
23.接（人）	jiē (rén)	to meet (a person)

補 充 詞

1.總機	zǒngjī	central exchange, telephone exchange, switchboard
2.分機	fēnjī	extension
3.佔線	zhàn xiàn	the line is busy (engaged), the number is engaged
4.打錯了	dǎ cuò le	(you have dialed the) wrong number
5.號碼	hàomǎ	number

(350, 351)

6.《人民日報》《Rénmín Rìbào》 "the People's Daily"

三、閱讀短文

看　報

帕蘭卡去找丁雲的時候，丁雲正在看報。她問丁雲："你在看什麼報？"

丁雲說："我在看《人民日報》，你來看，這兒有一條新聞，你們的一個友好代表團正在訪問中國。這兒還有他們參觀訪問的照片。"

帕蘭卡說："給我看看。"

這是五月二十七日的新聞，代表團在參觀北京的一個小學 (xiǎoxué, primary school)。這條新聞旁邊有三張照片。左邊的這張照片是代表團進教室的時候，孩子們正在上課。中間這張是他們跟孩子們一起玩兒呢。你看，他們正在唱歌、跳舞。右邊的那張是一個老師在給代表團介紹呢。

帕蘭卡說："這張報真有意思，給我好嗎？我媽媽很喜歡中國的孩子，給她看看中國孩子的照片，她一定很高興。"

"好，給你吧！"

"謝謝你，丁雲。"

(358, 359)

四、注釋 Notes

1. "請等一等"

"請等一等" has the same meaning as "請等等". When a monosyllabic verb is reduplicated, "一" can be inserted in between, e.g. "聽一聽", "走一走".

2. "你是帕蘭卡吧？"

The modal particle "吧" (2) often gives the statement a tone of uncertainty. If one forms an estimate of a thing, and yet is not very sure whether it is true, one can use "吧" at the end of the sentence. E.g.

這個漢字不對吧？

你們現在很忙吧？

她住 423 號吧？

3. "我在家裏。"

When the position word "裏邊" or "上邊" etc. is attached to a noun, "邊" is very often omitted, as in "城裏", "家裏", "桌子上", "報上", "城外", "國外" and "（工）廠外" etc.

4. "中國友好代表團正在參觀一個工廠。"

The object of the verb "訪問" may be either a thing or place or a person; the object of the verb "參觀" can only be a place or a thing other than a person. That's why you can't say "參觀某人", "參觀" means chiefly "看" though it is sometimes used in the sense of sightseeing. "訪問", on the other hand, is frequently used synonymously with "to interview".

5. "他怎麼樣？"

"How is he?"

"怎麼樣" is also a conversational greeting used between close acquaintances, e.g. "你怎麼樣？" "我很好".

6. "下午我給他打電的時候，他正上課呢。"

" …的時候 " is a common construction denoting time, meaning "when" or "at the time of". Like "以前" or " 以後", it is usually preceded by a word (e.g. "休息的時候"), a verbal construction (e.g. "參觀工廠的時候") or a subject-predicate construction.

7. "我說，明天你有空兒嗎？"

"我說" is a common expression used to introduce a new subject in a conversation or a telephone call.

五、替換與擴展 Substitution and Extension

(一)

1. 她在作什麼呢？

　她正在看電視呢。

　她跟誰一起看電視？

　她跟她妹妹一起看電視。

吃飯
喝茶
看《人民日報》
聽京劇

2. 他們在跳舞嗎？

　他們沒（有）跳舞，

　他們唱歌呢。

　（沒有，他們唱歌呢。）

工作，	玩兒
參觀工廠，	參觀學校
聽音樂，	聽新聞
復習課文，	看雜誌

3. 他們正在哪兒參觀呢?
   他們正在城裏參觀呢?

吃飯,	家裏
寫字,	桌子上
玩兒,	花園裏

4. 下午你給他打電話的時候，他作什麼呢?
   下午我給他打電話的時候，他正上課呢。

整理房間	給朋友寫信
睡覺	復習語法
洗澡	休息

5. 你看書的時候，你同學作什麼呢? 他在開車呢。

你去他家,	看電視
你找他,	接電話
你們訪問王先生,	學習漢語
你們出發,	穿大衣 *
你去郵局 *,	打電話

6. 請<u>等一等</u>，好嗎？
   好。

```
┌─────────────┐
│ 找    用    │
│ 看    聽    │
└─────────────┘
```

(二)

1. Making a telephone call

　　　　（Ａ打電話）

　　Ａ：喂，是外語學院總機＊嗎？

　　Ｂ：是啊。

　　Ａ：我要 262 分機＊。

　　Ｂ：現在佔線＊呢，請等一等。

　　Ａ：好。

　　　　　　＊　　　＊　　　＊

　　　　（Ａ接電話）

　　Ａ：喂？

　　Ｂ：是大光嗎？　我是王中啊。

　　Ａ：你找誰啊？

　　Ｂ：我找謝大光。

　　Ａ：這兒沒有謝大光，你打錯了＊。

　　Ｂ：對不起 (duì bu qǐ, sorry)。

　　　　　　＊　　　＊　　　＊

　　　　（Ａ接電話）

　　Ａ：喂？　誰啊？

B：我是王中，請問，謝大光在嗎?

A：他不在，他上課呢。有什麼事兒?

B：請你讓他今天晚上給我打個電話，好嗎?

A：好，你的電話號碼*是多少?

B：285742。謝謝你。

A：不謝。

2. Politely refusing

A：我用一用這本詞典好嗎?

B：對不起，我正用呢。下午給你吧。

A：好吧。

* * *

公用電話　　公共廁所

六、語法 Grammar

1. The progressive aspect of an action

(1) An action may be represented as being in progress, continuing or completed. To show that an action is in progress, place either one of the adverbs " 正在 ", " 正 " and " 在 " before the verb or " 呢 " at the end of the sentence. " 正在 ", " 正 " or " 在 " is very often used together with " 呢 " to express the progressive aspect. E.g.

Nouns or pronouns	Adverbs	Verbs	Nouns or pronouns	Particles
我	正在	看	電視	（呢）。
你	在	作	什麼	（呢）？
工人代表	正	歡迎	他們	（呢）。
我		聽	新聞	呢。
老師	（正）在	輔導	他們	呢？

"沒有" is used to make up the negative form of the progressive aspect. "沒有" may be shortened to "沒" if it goes before the verb. But at the end of the sentence or in short answers, "沒有" must be used in full. E.g.

他們在跳舞嗎？

——他們沒有跳舞，他們唱歌呢。

——他們沒跳舞，他們唱歌呢。

——沒有，他們唱歌呢。

——沒有。

(2) The aspect and the time (past, present or future) of an action are two different concepts. In Chinese the time of an action is expressed by means of time words. E.g.

他以前非常喜歡現代音樂。

我們今天參觀工廠。

(359, 360, 361)

我朋友明天來看我。

An action in progress may take place either in the present or in the past or future. E.g.

喂，你在作什麼呢？我在寫信呢。　(present)

下午他給我打電話的時候，我正看報呢。　(past)

明天晚上你去找他，他一定在看電視呢。　(future)

2. Elliptical questions formed with the modal particle "呢"

Elliptical questions may be formed by adding merely "呢" to a pronoun, noun or nominal construction. The meaning of this type of questions is determined mainly by the context. E.g.

你好嗎？

——我很好，你呢？（你好嗎？）

你在作什麼呢？

——我在復習課文呢，你呢？（你在作什麼呢？）

你現在有空兒嗎？

——我沒有空兒。

晚上呢？（晚上你有空兒嗎？）

When there is no context, elliptical questions of this type are usually used to ask where someone or something is. E.g.

古波呢？（古波在哪兒？）

你弟弟呢？（你弟弟在哪兒？）

我的筆呢？（我的筆在哪兒？）

3. Subject-predicate constructions as the attributive

When a subject-predicate construction is used attributively, there must be the structural particle "的" between the attributive and what it qualifies. E.g.

我給他打電話的時候，他正上課呢。

你看看我們參觀訪問的照片。

他買的椅子怎麼樣？

這是誰給你寫的信？

我們常去吃飯的餐廳在花園左邊。

七、練習 Exercises

1. Read out the following phrases:

友好代表團　　工人代表團　　銀行代表團
音樂代表團　　參觀工廠　　　參觀圖書館
參觀中文系　　參觀食堂　　　訪問中國
訪問工廠　　　訪問留學生　　訪問王先生
歡迎新同學　　歡迎你們　　　歡迎中國朋友
歡迎代表團　　打電話　　　　給朋友打電話
接電話

2. Complete the answers with sentences formed with "正在…呢" and the words or phrases given in brackets:

(1) A：帕蘭卡在家嗎？

B：在，＿＿＿＿＿＿＿。（吃飯）

(362, 363, 364)

(2) A：張先生現在忙不忙？

B：很忙，＿＿＿＿＿＿＿。（上課）

(3) A：請問，大夫呢？

B：在那兒，＿＿＿＿＿＿＿。（打電話）

(4) A：你的詞典呢？

B：我＿＿＿＿＿＿＿。（用）

(5) A：古波來不來？

B：他不來，＿＿＿＿＿＿＿。（參觀）

3. Make sentences with "正在…呢", using the verbs or verb-object constructions given below in the same way as the example:

Example　進食堂

吃飯

→我進食堂的時候，他正吃飯呢。

(1) 去閱覽室　　(2) 進商店　　　　(3) 給他打電話

看雜誌　　　　　　買東西　　　　　　復習

(4) 找他　　　　　(5) 回家

起床　　　　　　　喝咖啡

4. Say as much as you can about each of the following pictures:

① 　②

5. Insert the structural particle "的" where necessary in the following sentences:

    (1) 休息時候他常常聽音樂。

    (2) 參觀工廠人很多。

    (3) 這是媽媽給她襯衫。

    (4) 我買那本書很好。

    (5) 他認識新朋友是中國人。

6. Translate the followin into Chinese:
    (1) When I got to his place, he was watching TV.
    (2) When they started out, I was just getting up.
    (3) "Liuxuesheng" are students who study in a foreign country.
    (4) People who wait on tables in a cafe are called waiters.
    (5) The shop where he bought his clothes is not very large.
    (6) Who's the teacher who teaches you Chinese?

八、語音語調 Pronunciation and Intonation

1. Sense group stress (5)

    (1) To determine the sentence stress of a long sentence, divide the sentence into sense groups, then find out which syllable should receive stress. (In this book the sigh "∥" is used to mark out sense group.) E.g.

中國友好代表團∥正在參觀一個工廠。

你們的新聞代表團∥現在也在中國訪問呢。

(2) In sentences in which a prepositional construction is used adverbially and the verb is at the same time followed by an object, the objects of both the preposition and the verb are stressed, with the preposition pronounced with a weak stress. E.g.

下午我給古波打電話。

他在家裏看電視。

帕蘭卡跟丁雲一起去咖啡館。

2. Word stress (6)

When "一" is inserted between a pair of reduplicated monosyllabic verbs, it is pronounced in the neutral tone. The stress-pattern of this type of construction is "strong-weak-weak". E.g.

等一等 想一想 坐一坐 找一找

談一談 走一走 接一接 玩兒一玩兒

3. Exercises

Read out the following proverb:

Yìnián   zhī   jì   zàiyú   chūn,
一年   之   計   在於   春，
Yírì   zhī   jì   zàiyú   chén.
一日   之   計   在於   晨，

(The whole year's work depends on a good start in spring; the work for the day is best begun in the morning.)

第二十四課

復　習

一、課　文

媽 媽 作 的 點 心

古波的家在農村，他爸爸、媽媽都是農民。一天，他妹妹
Gǔbō de jiā zài nóngcūn, tā bàba, māma dōu shì nóngmín. Yìtiān, tā mèimei

安娜坐火車來學生城看他。安娜不認識古波的宿舍。這時候，
Ānnà zuò huǒchē lái xuésheng chéng kàn tā. Ānnà bú rènshi Gǔbō de sùshè.　Zhè shíhou,

旁邊有一個學生，他正在鍛鍊。安娜問他：“請問，這是六號
pángbiān yǒu yíge xuésheng, tā zhèngzài duànliàn. Ānnà wèn tā: "Qǐngwèn, zhè shì liùhào

宿舍嗎？”那個學生回答：“不，這是二號。六號在後邊，你
sùshè ma?"　　Nàge xuésheng huídá: "Bù, zhè shì èrhào.　Liùhào zài hòubiān, nǐ

跟我來。”安娜説：“謝謝你，我去找吧。”
gēn wǒ lái."　　Ānnà shuō:　"Xièxie nǐ, wǒ qù zhǎo ba."

安娜進宿舍的時候，古波正在復習漢語呢。古波説：“是
Ānnà jìn sùshè de shíhou, Gǔbō zhèngzài fùxí Hànyǔ ne. Gǔbō shuō: "Shì

你啊，安娜！我不知道你今天來。"
nǐ a, Ānnà! Wǒ bù zhīdao nǐ jīntiān lái."

"你怎麼樣，古波？"妹妹問。
"Nǐ zěnmeyàng, Gǔbō?" Mèimei wèn.

" 我很好。爸爸媽媽都好嗎？"
"Wǒ hěn hǎo. Bàba māma dōu hǎo ma?"

"他們都很好。看，這是媽媽給你們作的點心，那些點心
"Tāmen dōu hěn hǎo. Kàn, zhè shì māma gěi nǐmen zuò de diǎnxin, nàxiē diǎnxin

是給丁雲的。"
shì gěi Dīng Yún de."

" 太好了，你回家的時候謝謝媽媽。"
"Tài hǎo le, nǐ huí jiā de shíhou xièxie māma."

" 這是漢語書嗎？我看看。"安娜說，" 漢語一定很難吧？"
"Zhè shì Hànyǔ shū ma? Wǒ kànkan." Ānnà shuō, "Hànyǔ yídìng hěn nán ba?"

古波告訴她，漢語語法不太難，漢字很難。他很喜歡寫漢
Gǔbō gàosu tā, Hànyǔ yǔfǎ bú tài nán, Hànzì hěn nán. Tā hěn xǐhuan xiě Hàn-

字。他現在很忙，每天都學習生詞、念課文、寫漢字，晚上還
zì. Tā xiànzài hěn máng, měi tiān dōu xuéxí shēngcí, niàn kèwén, xiě Hànzì, wǎnshang hái

作練習。每天都十一點睡覺。
zuò liànxí. Měi tiān dōu shíyīdiǎn shuì jiào.

"你們的中國老師叫什麼？"安娜問。
"Nǐmen de Zhōngguó lǎoshī jiào shénme?" Ānnà wèn.

"我們的中國老師叫王書文。上課的時候他很認真，常常
"Wǒmen de Zhōngguó lǎoshī jiào Wáng Shūwén. Shàng kè de shíhou tā hěn rènzhēn, cháng-

問我們懂不懂，有沒有問題。下課以後還跟我們一起說漢語。
cháng wèn wǒmen dǒng bu dǒng, yǒu méi yǒu wèntí. Xià kè yǐhòu hái gēn wǒmen yìqǐ shuō Hànyǔ.

我們也常常去他那兒玩兒。"
Wǒmen yě chángcháng qù tā nàr wánr."

二、生　詞

1.點心	diǎnxin	light refreshments, pastry
2.農村	nóngcūn	countryside, rural areas
3.農民	nóngmín	peasant
4.火車	huǒchē	train
5.鍛鍊	duànliàn	to do physical training
6.回答	huídá	to reply, to answer
7.些	xiē	a measure word, some
8.難	nán	difficult
9.生詞	shēngcí	new word
詞	cí	word
10.念	niàn	to read aloud

(374, 375)

11.練習	liànxí	exercise, to practise
12.認真	rènzhēn	conscientious, serious, in earnest
13.懂	dǒng	to understand

專　名

| 1.安娜 | Ānnà | a personal name |
| 2.王書文 | Wáng Shūwén | a personal name |

三、注釋 Notes

1. "一天，他妹妹安娜坐火車來學生城看他。"

"一天" means "a certain day", usually used to denote an indefinite time in a past event, that is, not necessary to specify.

2. "我不知道你今天來。"

"I didn't know you would come today."

In "我不知道你今天來", the subject-predicate construction "你今天來" functions as the object of the verb "知道".

3. "那些點心是給丁雲的。"

"些" is a measure word showing an indefinite quantity and is usually used after "這", "那" or "哪" to qualify nouns, e.g. "這些書", "那些工人".

"些" is used in combination with "一" only, and never with any other numerals, e.g. "一些點心", "一些報".

四、看圖會話 Talk about These Pictures

1. Making an appointment

現在你有事兒嗎?
你什麼時候有空兒?
……好嗎?

2. Entertaining a guest

請吃……
你要……還是……?

3. Shopping

你要什麼?
有……嗎?
還要什麼?

4. Offering congratulations

祝賀你!

5. Asking the age

(1) 他多大歲數?
(2) 你今年幾歲?

6. Asking the way

(1) ……在哪兒?
(2) 哪兒是……?
(3) 這兒有……嗎?

7. Asking for opinions from others

　(1)　喜歡不喜歡……?

　(2)　……有沒有意思?

　(3)　……怎麼樣?

8. Making a telephone call

　(1)　……在嗎?

　(2)　你是……嗎?

　(3)　請你告訴他……

9. Presenting a gift

這是給你的……

五、語法小結　A Brief Summary of Grammar

1. The six types of questions

(1) Questions with " 嗎 "

Of all the six types of questions, the kind formed with " 嗎 " is the most extensively used to ask about something about which the speaker has no foreknowledge and for which he expects neither an affirmative nor negative answer.

你媽媽是大夫嗎?

您忙嗎？

（你）不想你的男朋友嗎？

(2) Affirmative-negative questions

This type of questions is also the most commonly used. Questions formed with "嗎" can all be turned into affirmative-negative questions.

他有沒有妹妹？

你認識不認識她？

你們的食堂大不大？

(3) Questions with an interrogative pronoun

Questions with an interrogative pronoun are used to ask about "誰", "什麼", "哪", "哪兒", "怎麼辦", "多少" and "幾". Note that "嗎" is never used at the end of this type of question:

今天星期幾？

我們的新房子怎麼樣？

你今年多大？

(4) Alternative questions with "還是"

This kind of questions is used when two or more different answers may be expected.

你喜歡古典音樂還是喜歡現代音樂？

他是英國人還是法國人？

他下午去圖書館還是晚上去圖書館？

(5) Tag questions with "是嗎" (or "是不是" or "對嗎")

Questions of such kind are used when the speaker forms an estimate of a thing which is necessarily confirmed.

中國人喜歡喝茶，是嗎？

這個電影很有意思，是不是？

Tag questions with "好嗎" are usually used as a form of polite request when one makes proposals and asks the person thus addressed if he is agreeable or not.

我們去咖啡館，好嗎?

請您參加舞會，好嗎?

(6) Elliptical questions with "呢"

This is a most simple type of question, used mainly in colloquial speech. E.g.

我很好，你呢?

我在看電視，你呢?

你的照片呢?

2. Attributives and the structural particle "的" (2)

(1) Used attributively, a disyllabic adjective as a rule takes "的" after it.

這個年輕的大夫叫什麼?

她是一個認真的學生。

(2) Used attributively, a verb usually takes "的" after it.

參觀的人很多。

休息的時候，他常常去鍛鍊。

(3) Used attributively, a verbal construction must take "的" after it.

這是送她的花兒。

給女兒買的裙子真漂亮。

(4) Used attributively, a subject-predicate construction must take "的" after it.

他給我一張他們參觀工廠的照片。

帕蘭卡給他打電話的時候，他正看報呢。

3. Word order of a series of attributives

When a noun has more than one attributive, possessive nouns or pronouns are always placed at the head of the series. Adjective or noun modifiers are usually placed closest to the head word. Demonstrative pronouns usually precede numeral-measure words. E.g.

那兩本雜誌

他的那兩本雜誌

他的那兩本中文雜誌

他的那兩本新中文雜誌

六、練習 Exercises

1. Write out the numerals in Chinese characters and give a measure word for each of the nouns:

(6)	班	(12)	同學
(10)	啤酒	(3)	咖啡
(62)	工人	(85)	農民
(4)	代表團	(7)	問題
(4)	照片	(11)	票
(5)	房間	(8)	襯衫
(32)	字	(26)	詞

（ 1 ） 圖書館	（ 1 ） 花兒
（22） 桌子	（ 3 ） 裙子
（ 9 ） 工廠	（15） 服務員

2. Change the following to different types of questions (Nos. 2 and 9 are not changed to affirmative-negative questions):

(1) 今天二十七號。

(2) 他從農村來。

(3) 這是給我朋友的信。

(4) 圖書館在食堂旁邊。

(5) 我們班星期三去城外。

(6) 我家有一個小花園。

(7) 他每天復習課文。

(8) 這個代表團不大。

(9) 她在等我呢。

(10) 那本雜誌很新。

3. Analyze the following sentences, pointing out the subject, main element of the predicate, object, attributive and adverbial adjunct:

(1) 老師問的問題不太難。

(2) 他在看今天的報呢。

(3) 這是他寫的漢字嗎?

(4) 我聽他們唱歌。

(5) 爸爸給他的襯衫很漂亮。

(6) 他知道今天不上課。

(7) 那些都是我買的點心。

(8) 一個從中國來的代表團在參觀這個工廠。

(384, 385)

4. Fill in the blanks without referring to the text until you finish these sentences:

(1) 安娜是古波 _____ ，她 _____ 歲。她 _____ 農村來看哥哥。

(2) 古波 _____ 學生城住，他現在很 _____ 。他不常常 _____ 家看爸爸媽媽，他不知道安娜 _____ 。

(3) 安娜 _____ 時候，古波正 _____ 漢語呢。他每天都 _____ 生詞、_____ 課文、_____ 練習。

(4) 安娜不 _____ 漢語、也不 _____ 漢字。她問古波，漢語 _____ 不 _____ ？

(5) 王老師是一個 _____ 的老師，他教 _____ 課。他非常 _____ ，_____ 以後還常常 _____ 學生學習。同學們都 _____ 他。

5. Correct the following erroneous sentences:

(1) 帕蘭卡去古波宿舍在星期五。

(2) 九月四號一九七九年他去中國。

(3) 我們班有十四學生。

(4) 那個天我跟他一起去看電影。

(5) 左邊的本畫報是我的。

(6) 我很喜歡這些五個歌兒。

(7) 他復習復習課文的時候，我正鍛鍊呢。

(8) 今天他很高興不高興？

(9) 這些生詞難的。

(10) 他寫漢字很好。

(11) 我回答問題老師問。

⑿ 他住房間 125 號。

⒀ 我們問他介紹介紹漢語語法。

⒁ 他是很認真的一個老師。

⒂ 晚上我去看一個我朋友。

⒃ 那件她的襯衫很漂亮。

第二十五課

一、課　文

他 作 飯 作 得 好 不 好

帕蘭卡：我們來得太晚了，在哪兒停車呢？
Palanka:　Wǒmen lái de tài wǎn le, zài nǎr tíng chē ne?

古　　波：這兒好。前邊是條河，在這兒停車吧？
Gubo:　Zhèr hǎo. Qiánbiān shì tiáo hé, zài zhèr tíng chē ba?

帕蘭卡：好。我和丁雲去游泳，你準備吃的，好嗎？
Palanka:　Hǎo. Wǒ hé Dīng Yún qù yóu yǒng, nǐ zhǔnbèi chī de, hǎo ma?

古　　波：好吧。我去釣魚，請你們喝魚湯。
Gubo:　Hǎo ba. Wǒ qù diào yú, qǐng nǐmen hē yú tāng.

＊　　　　　＊　　　　　＊

古　　波：兩位小姐，来吧。
Gubo:　Liǎngwèi xiǎojie, lái ba.

帕蘭卡：等一等，我們在休息呢。
Palanka:　Děngyideng, wǒmen zài xiūxi ne.

古　波：丁雲游泳游得怎麼樣？
Gubo: Dīng Yún yóu yǒng yóu de zěnmeyàng?

帕蘭卡：她游得真快。
Palanka: Tā yóu de zhēn kuài.

丁　雲：哪裏，我游得很慢。你游得好。
Ding Yun: Nǎli, wǒ yóu de hěn màn. Nǐ yóu de hǎo.

帕蘭卡：古波是我的教練，他教我教得很好。
Palanka: Gǔbō shì wǒ de jiàoliàn, tā jiāo wǒ jiāo de hěn hǎo.

丁　雲：古波作飯作得好不好？
Ding Yun: Gǔbō zuò fàn zuò de hǎo bu hǎo?

帕蘭卡：他魚湯作得不錯。來，請吃吧！
Palanka: Tā yú tāng zuò de búcuò. Lái, qǐng chī ba!

古　波：丁雲，給你麵包、火腿。
Gubo: Dīng Yún, gěi nǐ miànbāo, huǒtuǐ.

帕蘭卡：我要點兒奶酪。
Palanka: Wǒ yào diǎnr nǎilào.

古　波：好。丁雲，再吃點兒吧！
Gubo: Hǎo. Dīng Yún, zài chī diǎnr ba!

丁　雲：謝謝，我吃得不少了。我要點兒湯。
Ding Yun: Xièxie, wǒ chī de bù shǎo le. Wǒ yào diǎnr tāng.

　　　　　　　(391, 392)

古 波：請你們喝——
Gubo: Qǐng nǐmen hē ——

帕蘭卡：魚湯？
Palanka: Yú tāng?

古 波：不，喝礦泉水。
Gubo: Bù, hē kuàngquánshuǐ.

二、生　詞

1.得	de	a structural particle
2.晚	wǎn	late
3.停	tíng	to stop, to come to a stop
4.前邊	qiánbiān	front
5.河	hé	river
6.游泳	yóu yǒng	to swim, swimming
7.準備	zhǔnbèi	to prepare
8.釣	diào	to fish with a hook and bait
9.魚	yú	fish
10.湯	tāng	soup
11.位	wèi	a measure word
12.快	kuài	fast, quick
13.哪裏	nǎli	it is nothing

14.慢	màn	slow
15.教練	jiàoliàn	coach, trainer
16.不錯	búcuò	correct, right, not bad, pretty good
17.麵包	miànbāo	bread
18.火腿	huǒtuǐ	ham
19.一點兒	yìdiǎnr	a little, a bit
20.奶酪	nǎilào	cheese
21.再	zài	again, once more, a second time
22.礦泉水	kuàngquánshuǐ	mineral water

補 充 詞

1.清楚	qīngchu	clear, distinct
2.流利	liúlì	fluent
3.整齊	zhěngqí	tidy
4.菜	cài	dish
5.餃子	jiǎozi	Chinese dumpling
6.雞蛋	jīdàn	chicken egg
7.牛奶	niúnǎi	(cow's) milk
8.比較	bǐjiào	comparatively, to compare
9.條	tiáo	measure word (for river); see page 141

(394, 402)

三、閱讀短文

古波的日記 (rìjì, diary)

七月二十四日　星期六

今天是星期六，下午我跟帕蘭卡、比里一起到王老師那兒。王老師正在看書。他看見 (kànjiàn, to see)我們來，非常高興。他問我們，現在忙不忙？課文復習得怎麼樣？他教得快不快？我們告訴他，現在課文比較難，生詞也很多，我們比較忙。

王老師說，這學期(xuéqī, term)我們學習得都很認真，學得很好。帕蘭卡漢字寫得很清楚，上課的時候她回答問題回答得很對。比里語法學得很好。我漢語說得比較流利。他讓我們互相學習，互相幫助。

王老師問我們："你們每天都鍛鍊嗎？"帕蘭卡說她不常鍛鍊。他問我們每天幾點睡覺。我告訴他，我十二點半睡覺。比里說他十二點睡。王老師說："你們睡得太晚。"

五點半，王老師還不讓我們走。他說："你們在這兒吃飯吧，我們一起包 (bāo, to make) 餃子。"中國餃子真不錯，我們都吃得不少。

四、注釋 Notes

1. "來得太晚了。" "吃得不少了。"

" 了 " here is a modal particle used to indicate the affirmative attitude of the speaker towards what has happened.

2. "在哪兒停車呢？"

The modal particle " 呢 " (1) can be added at the end of a question with an interrogative pronoun, an affirmative-negative question or an alternative question with " 還是 " to soften the tone. E.g.

我們幾點出發呢？

他懂不懂這課語法呢？

你現在去鍛鍊，還是下午去鍛鍊呢？

3. "兩位小姐，來吧！"

The measure word " 位 " applies to persons only. It is more respectful, courteous or polite than the measure word " 個 ". But Gubo is using the word jocularly here.

4. "哪裡，我游得很慢。"

" 哪裡 " is an interrogative pronoun having the same meaning as " 哪兒 ". But here it has a negative meaning, used to reply to a complimentary remark, implying that the speaker does not at all deserve the praise.

5. "我要點兒奶酪。"

" 一點兒 ", a measure word, indicates an indefinite small quantity (usually smaller than that " 一些 " indicates). When it appears at any place in a sentence except the beginning, " 一 " can be omitted.

" 一點兒 " is more often than not used to qualify a noun. The noun can be omitted if the reference is clear.

(395, 396)

6. "再吃點兒吧！"

The adverb "再" (1) usually indicates that an action is going to be continued or repeated some time in the future.

五、替換與擴展 Substitution and Extension

(一)

1. 他來得晚嗎？
   他來得不晚。

說，	快
走，	慢
念，	好
起，	晚
學，	認真

2. 你朋友工作得怎麼樣？
   他工作得很好。

休息，	好
回答，	對
復習，	慢
準備，	認真
介紹，	清楚*

3. 丁雲在作什麼？
   她在游泳呢。
   她游得怎麼樣？

她游得不錯。

白老師，	上課
帕蘭卡，	跳舞
古波，	開車
那位小姐，	學漢語
那位太太，	整理房間

看書，	認真
用紙，	多
寫字，	好看
念生詞，	對
說漢語，	流利*
念課文，	清楚*

4. 他作飯作得好不好?
他作飯作得很好。

電影票，	買，	多
語法，	學，	好
問題，	回答，	快
生詞，	學，	多
漢字，	寫，	整齊*
課文，	念，	流利*

5. 你漢字寫得快不快?
我漢字寫得不太快。

(398, 399)

6. 老師讓誰説英語?

　　老師讓他説英語。

　　英語他説得怎麼樣?

　　英語他説得很慢。

念，	課文
寫，	漢字
作，	今天的練習
回答，	這些問題

7. 再吃點兒麵包吧!

　　謝謝，我吃得不少了。

吃，	火腿
吃，	菜
吃，	餃子*
吃，	鷄蛋*
喝，	湯
喝，	牛奶*

(二)

1. Compliment and reply

　　A：你是中文系的學生吧?

　　B：是啊，我正學習中文呢。

　　A：你説漢語説得很流利。

　　B：哪裡，我説得不太好。

　　A：這是你寫的漢字嗎? 寫得真漂亮。

　　B：我寫得很慢，以後請多幫助。

2. Asking for information

A：你知道哪兒作裙子作得好？

B：我給你介紹一家，大商店旁邊那家作得好。

A：謝謝你，我去看一看。

3. Exchanging amenities

A：昨天你休息得好嗎？

B：很好，你呢？

A：昨天晚上我睡得不太好，今天起得很晚。

4. Entertaining a guest

A：菜*作得不好，你們都吃得很少。

B：哪裡，太太，您的魚湯作得真好，我非常喜歡喝。

A：你再喝點兒吧！

B：謝謝，我喝得不少了。

*　　　*　　　*

六、語法 Grammar

1. Complement of degree
A verb or an adjective can take after it another word to explain further
or complete its meaning, which is known as a complement. Complements

(400, 401, 403)

that indicate the degree or extent of the quality or character of the action denoted by the verb or of the state denoted by the adjective are called complements of degree. Simple complements of degree are usually made of adjectives and the structural particle "得" is used to connect the verb and its complement of degree.

Complements of degree are usually used to indicate either actions that have already come true or actions that are habitually frequent.

The negative form of a sentence with a verbal predicate containing a complement of degree is made by adding "不" before the complement and never before the verb. The affirmative-negative form of this type of sentence is made by juxtaposing the affirmative and negative forms of the complement of degree.

Nouns or pronouns	Verbs	"得"	Adverbs	Adjectives	Particle
他	來	得	很	晚。	
她	唱	得	不	好。	
你	休息	得		好	嗎?
你	休息	得		怎麼樣?	
你	休息	得		好不好?	

When a verb takes an object and is followed at the same time by a complement of degree, the verb must be repeated after the object before "得" and the complement of degree are added to it.

Nouns or pro-nouns	Verbs	Nouns	Verbs (re-peated)	"得"	Adverbs	Adjectives	Particle
他	作	飯	作	得	很	好。	
我	寫	漢字	寫	得	不太	快。	
你	回答	問題	回答	得		對	嗎?
你	回答	問題	回答	得		怎麼樣?	
你	回答	問題	回答	得		對不對?	

2. Preposed object

The object may be placed before the verb, or even before the subject to make it emphatic and conspicuous or when the object is long and involved. When a sentence containing a complement of degree has its object placed before the verb or the subject, it will no longer be necessary to repeat the verb. E.g.

他車開得很好。

老師的問題你回答得很對，也很快。

那些生詞他用得怎麼樣?

When the verb takes an object and is followed at the same time by a complement of degree, the sentence can be arranged in the following three ways:

他學外語學得很快。

他外語學得很快。

外語他學得很快。

(405, 406)

七、練習 Exercises

1. Read out the following phrases:

來得很晚　　　來得真晚　　　走得不快

走得不太晚　寫得很快　　　寫得真慢

穿得不多　　　穿得不太好　看得很多

看得真快　　　念得不少　　　念得不太對

說得很對　　　說得真有意思

學得不錯　　　學得不太快　教得很認真

教得真快　　　開得不快　　　開得不太慢

介紹得很少　介紹得真多　準備得不好

準備得不太認真　　　回答得多

回答得真快　　　　　整理得不慢

整理得不太好

2. Complete the following sentences with complements of degree:

    (1) 他玩兒 _____ 。

    (2) 張老師教 _____ 。

    (3) 古波說漢語 _____ 。

    (4) 丁雲游泳 _____ 。

    (5) 他們法語 _____ 。

    (6) 我們問題 _____ 。

3. Complete the following dialogues:

    (1) A：_____ ？

    　　 B：他寫漢字寫得很好看。

(2)　A：＿＿＿＿＿＿？

　　　B：我開車開得不快也不慢。

(3)　A：＿＿＿＿＿＿？

　　　B：他跳舞跳得很好。

(4)　A：＿＿＿＿＿＿？

　　　B：那個學生來得不晚。

(5)　A：請您再吃點兒。

　　　B：謝謝，我吃得＿＿＿＿＿。

4. Make sentences in the same way as the example given:
Example

　　　作飯　　　好

　→你作飯作得好不好？

　　我作飯作得不太好。

　　誰作飯作得好？

　　他作飯作得很好。

(1) 睡覺　　　晚　　　(5) 休息　　　好

(2) 作練習　快　　　(6) 看書　　　多

(3) 念課文　慢　　　(7) 寫信　　　少

(4) 起床　　　晚　　　(8) 復習語法　認真

5. Ask each other questions about each of the following pictures, using complements of degree:

(1)　　　　　　(2)　　　　　　(3)

　　　　　　(407, 408, 409)

(4)   (5)   (6)

八、語音語調　　**Pronunciation and Intonation**

1.　Sentence tunes (1)

In Chinese, there are two basic sentence tunes: high-pitch and low-pitch. One characteristic of Chinese sentence tunes is that the pitch, whether high or low, is kept up throughout the sentence. In a sentence uttered in high-pitch tune the pitch goes steadily up, while for a low-pitch tune sentence the pitch goes steadily down. But no matter which tune is used, all syllables forming the sentence must be pronounced in their original tone.

The rise or fall that terminates the two sentence tunes is most clearly indicated by non-neutral syllables at the end of the sentence. The high-pitch sentence tune ends in a rising intonation, but sometimes in a falling intonation as well. The low-pitch sentence tune ends in a falling intonation, but sometimes in a rising intonation as well.

(1)　Questions with "嗎" are said in the high-pitch tune (in this book, the tone-graph above the dotted line indicates that the sentence should be said in the high-pitch sentence tune) and end in a rising intonation (marked with the sign " ⌒ " in this book). E.g.

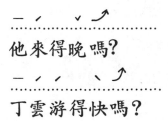

他來得晚嗎?

丁雲游得快嗎?

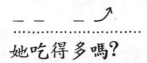

她吃得多嗎?

(2) Declarative sentences are said in the low-pitch sentence tune (the tone-graph is placed under the dotted line), and end in a falling intonation (marked with sigh " ↘ "). E.g.

他來得很晚。

他教我教得很好。

我請你們喝魚湯。

(3) In affirmative-negative questions containing a complement of degree, the affirmative part of the complement is stressed, and the negative is pronounced with a weak stress. The structural particle "得" is pronounced in the neutral tone. A pause is usually allowed after "得", but there should be no pause between the verb and "得". The whole sentence is said in the high-pitch sentence tune and ends in a falling intonation. E.g.

他作飯作得好不好?

丁雲游泳游得快不快?

她寫字寫得好看不好看?

(410, 411, 412)

2. Exercises

Read the following words and expressions containing the sounds s and sh, paying special attention to the pronunciation of these two sounds:

送花—老師　　食堂—宿舍

告訴—書房　　臥室—三層

礦泉水—四十四　生詞—四十

Read out the following proverbs:

Sāntiān dǎ yú, liǎngtiān shài wǎng.
三天 打 魚， 兩天 曬 網。

(Go fishing for three days and dry the nets for two; lack perseverance)

Zhàn de gāo, kàn de yuǎn.
站 得 高， 看 得 遠。

(Stand on a high plane and see far ahead.)

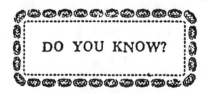

DO YOU KNOW?

Loanwords in Chinese

There are a great number of loanwords in Chinese one of which in common use is " 葡萄 ". It was introduced into China about two thousand years ago at the same time as the introduction of the grape plant itself. Since the nineteenth century, a great many foreign words, mostly those used in social and natural sciences, have been loaned from other languages, notably English.

Loanwords in modern Chinese fall into two classes: 1, those transliterations of whole words, e.g. "葡萄" and "咖啡", 2, partial transliterations coupled with a Chinese character that indicates the meaning of the loanword, e.g. "啤酒". Loanwords of the latter class conform better to the speech habits of the native speakers of Chinese.

第二十六課

一、課　文

我要研究中國文學

古　波：我們走吧。
Gubo:　Wǒmen zǒu ba.

帕蘭卡：還早呢，我要再跟丁雲談談。丁雲，你會說英語和法
Palanka:　Hái zǎo ne, wǒ yào zài gēn Dīng Yún tántan. Dīng Yún, nǐ huì shuō Yīngyǔ hé Fǎ-

　　　　語，你以後想作什麼工作？
　　　　yǔ, nǐ yǐhòu xiǎng zuò shénme gōngzuò?

丁　雲：我想當翻譯。你呢？
Ding Yun:　Wǒ xiǎng dāng fānyi. Nǐ ne?

帕蘭卡：我也想當翻譯。翻譯工作能加深兩國人民的了解。
Palanka:　Wǒ yě xiǎng dāng fānyi. Fānyi gōngzuò néng jiāshēn liǎngguó rénmín de liǎojiě.

丁　雲：你說得真對。古波，你想作什麼工作呢？
Ding Yun:　Nǐ shuō de zhēn duì. Gūbō, nǐ xiǎng zuò shénme gōngzuò ne?

古　波：我不想當翻譯。我要研究中國文學。中國有很多有名
Gubo: Wǒ bù xiǎng dāng fānyì. Wǒ yào yánjiū Zhōngguó wénxué. Zhōngguó yǒu hěn duō yǒumíng

　　　　的作家。
　　　　de zuòjiā.

丁　雲：你要研究哪位作家？
Ding Yun: Nǐ yào yánjiū nǎwèi zuòjiā?

古　波：魯迅或者郭沫若。
Gubo: Lǔ Xùn huòzhě Guō Mòruò.

帕蘭卡：今年我們就想去中國學習。
Palanka: Jīnnián wǒmen jiù xiǎng qù Zhōngguó xuéxí.

丁　雲：你們學得不錯，應該去。今年能不能去？
Ding Yun: Nǐmen xué de búcuò, yīnggāi qù. Jīnnián néng bu néng qù?

帕蘭卡：我們倆都能去。
Palanka: Wǒmen liǎ dōu néng qù.

丁　雲：太好了，在那兒你們能學得更好。回國以後，可以找
Ding Yun: Tài hǎo le, zài nàr nǐmen néng xué de gèng hǎo. Huí guó yǐhòu, kěyǐ zhǎo

　　　　一個理想的工作。
　　　　yíge lǐxiǎng de gōngzuò.

古　波：可是這很不容易啊！
Gubo: Kěshì zhè hěn bù róngyì a!

丁　雲："有志者事竟成"，這是中國的成語。

Ding Yun: "Yǒuzhìzhěshìjìngchéng", Zhè shì Zhōngguó de chéngyǔ.

二、生　詞

1.研究	yánjiū	to research
2.文學	wénxué	literature
3.早	zǎo	early
4.談	tán	to talk, to chat
5.會	huì	can, to know how to
6.當	dāng	to serve as, to act as
7.翻譯	fānyi	interpreter, translator, to interpret, to translate
8.能	néng	can, to be able to
9.加深	jiāshēn	to deepen
10.人民	rénmín	people
11.了解	liǎojiě	to understand, to know
12.有名	yǒumíng	famous, well-known
13.作家	zuòjiā	writer
14.或者	huòzhě	or
15.就	jiù	at once, right away
16.應該	yīnggāi	should, ought to
17.倆	liǎ	a numeral-measure word, two, both

18.可以	kěyǐ	may
19.理想	lǐxiǎng	ideal
20.可是	kěshì	but
21.容易	róngyi	easy
22.有志者事竟成	yǒuzhìzhě-shìjìngchéng	Where there is a will, there is a way.
23.成語	chéngyǔ	proverb, idiom

專　　名

| 1.魯迅 | Lǔ Xùn | Lu Xun |
| 2.郭沫若 | Guō Mòruò | Guo Moruo |

補　充　詞

1.歌劇	gējù	opera
2.小説	xiǎoshuō	a novel, fiction
3.詩歌	shīgē	poem
4.畫	huà	to paint, to draw
5.畫兒	huàr	painting, drawing, picture
6.晚飯	wǎnfàn	supper
7.進來	jìn lái	to come in, to enter
8.唱片	chàngpiàn	phonograph records

三、閱讀短文

聯　歡

　　星期六晚上，中文系的同學要跟中國留學生聯歡 (liánhuān, get-together)，同學們都知道帕蘭卡和古波很喜歡中國音樂，讓他們準備一個中國歌兒。他們問帕蘭卡能不能用中文唱，她說她可以跟古波一起唱。

　　"我們唱什麼歌兒呢？"古波問帕蘭卡。

　　"丁雲很會唱歌兒。我們去問問她，好嗎？"帕蘭卡說。

　　丁雲知道他們要參加聯歡，還要唱中國歌兒，她非常高興。她說："你們倆唱一個《洪湖水，浪打浪》（《Hónghú Shuǐ, Làng Dǎ Làng》，The Honghu Lake Waters Surge in Majestic Waves ）吧。"

　　帕蘭卡請丁雲介紹這個歌兒。丁雲告訴他們，這個歌兒是中國的一個有名的歌劇裏邊的。古波問丁雲有沒有這個歌兒的唱片，丁雲說她有，她請他們聽這張唱片。

　　古波和帕蘭卡都說這個歌兒很好。帕蘭卡問丁雲："現在你有空兒嗎？你能不能教我們？"

　　丁雲說："可以。我應該幫助你們，我們一起唱吧。這個歌兒不太難，你們一定能唱得很好。"

四、注釋 Notes

1. "還早呢。"

"It's still early."

The adverb "還" (2) indicates the existence of a phenomenon or the continuation of an action.

2. "我要研究魯迅或者郭沫若。"

The conjunctions "或者" and "還是" are both used to connect clauses suggesting two alternatives or possibilities. "或者" is mostly used in statements and "還是" in alternative questions.

3. "今年我們就想去中國學習。"

The adverb "就" (1) very often indicates something happens early, soon, quickly or imminently. Here "就" is used to signify the eagerness of those students to go and study Chinese in China.

4. "我們倆都能去。"

"倆" is a colloquialism used to refer to two persons, as in "我們倆", "你們倆" and "他們倆". "倆" usually takes no measure word after it.

5. "可是這很不容易啊！"

"可是" is an adversative conjunction used to indicate contrast of ideas. "這" refers to the foregoing statement "找一個理想的工作".

五、替換與擴展　Substitution and Extension

㈠

1. 你想當老師嗎？

我很想當老師。

| 學習文學 |
| 參觀工廠 |
| 去鍛鍊 |
| 了解那個作家 |
| 看歌劇* |

　　　　　(422, 423, 424)

2. 他要研究中國音樂嗎?
   他不想研究中國音樂,
   他要研究中國文學。

```
聽京劇,        聽民歌
喝啤酒,        喝礦泉水
進城,          回家
釣魚,          游泳
買麵包,        買火腿
翻譯小説*,     翻譯詩歌*
```

3. 他會不會説法語?
   他會説法語。
   他説得怎麼樣?
   他説得很好。

```
開車
游泳
寫這個漢字
念那些生詞
作今天的練習
畫* 畫兒*
```

4. 你能不能翻譯這個成語?
   我不能,他能翻譯。

```
翻譯這本書
看《人民日報》*
教他們英語
當教練
回答他的問題
```

5. 明天你能<u>來上課</u>嗎?
　　明天我能來上課。
　　你能不能八點來?
　　可以。

去參觀工廠
來接你朋友
參加舞會
去城外玩兒
幫助我
來吃晚飯＊

6. 可以<u>問問題</u>嗎?
　　可以，請吧。

用一用這個電話
坐你的車
從這兒走
在這兒坐一坐
吸煙

(二)

1.　Talking about plans

　　A：明天你想作什麼?

　　B：我想在家休息，你想去哪兒?

　　A：我想進城看電影。

2.　Making an appointment

　　A：你好。星期六我想請你吃晚飯＊，你能來嗎?

　　B：謝謝你，我很想來，可是星期六晚上我有點事兒。

A：星期天怎麼樣?

B：那好，我一定來。幾點?

A：七點。你太太能來嗎?

B：能來，她很想看看你們。

A：那太好了。

3. Asking permission

A：可以進來* 嗎?

B：請等一等。

......

好，請進。

*　　*　　*

A：先生，我能聽您的課嗎?

B：你是不是這兒的學生?

A：不是。我是大夫，今天我要去中國
　　訪問。我想聽您的漢語課，可以嗎?

B：可以，歡迎你來。

A：謝謝。

4. Prohibitions

A：先生，閱覽室裏不能吸煙，您要吸煙，
　　請在外邊吸吧。

B：好，對不起。

*　　*　　*

| 請 勿 吸 煙
QING WU XI YAN | 謝 絕 參 觀
XIE JUE CAN GUAN | 禁 止 停 車
JIN ZHI TING CHE |

六、語法 Grammar

Optative verbs

Optative verbs such as "想", "要", "會", "能", "可以" and "應該" are more often than not used before verbs to express ability, possibility or intention or wishes. Optative verbs are made negative by means of "不" except in a few very special cases. The affirmative-negative form of sentences with optative verbs is usually made by juxtaposing the affirmative and negative forms of the optative verbs.

Nouns or pronouns	Adverb	Optative verbs	Verbs	Nouns or pronouns	Particle
古波 你 他 你	不	要 想 會 能 不 能	研究 當 開 來?	中國文學。 老師 車。	嗎?

1. "要" and "想" are both verbs (See Lessons 19 and 14), and optative verbs as well. As optative verbs, they both indicate volition or intention, but "要" (its negative form is "不想") emphasizes one's strong will or desire to do something while "想" emphasizes one's plan or wish. E.g.

① 同志，我要買那本書。

(428, 430, 431)

同志，我想買本字典，你們這兒有嗎？

② 星期天你想進城嗎？

我不想去，我要回家。

2. "會" is an optative verb as well as an ordinary verb. As an optative verb, "會" denotes skill acquired or mastered as a result of study. E.g.

你會不會游泳？

他不會說英語。

這個練習我不會作，請你幫助幫助我。

3. The optative verbs "能" and "可以" are both used to express ability to do something. E.g.

他現在能看中文雜誌。

每星期你能學幾課？

我可以翻譯這本書。

"能" and "可以" may also be used to express ability or lack of it depending on circumstances. E.g.

你們今年能不能去？

可以進來嗎？

閱覽室裏不能吸煙。

"不可以" usually expresses prohibition. "不能", the negative form of both "能" and "可以", indicates inability to do something.

4. The optative verb "應該" indicates need arising from moral or factual necessity. E.g.

(432, 433)

你們學得不錯，應該去中國。

你們學習漢語，應該會說、會聽、會寫。

Notice that optative verbs can never be reduplicated, nor can they be followed by modal particles.

七、練習 Exercises

1. Read out the following phrases:

加深了解　　　加深認識　　　了解中國

了解他們　　　中國人民　　　兩國人民

《人民日報》　《人民畫報》　研究文學

研究音樂　　　研究語法　　　研究問題

有名的作家　　有名的電影　　有名的大夫

有名的工廠　　理想的工作　　理想的房子

理想的朋友　　我的理想

2. Answer the following questions in the negative:

(1) 他會不會說漢語？

(2) 她能參加晚上的舞會嗎？

(3) 你要不要喝咖啡？

(4) 這兒可以不可以游泳？

(5) 明天你能跟我們一起進城嗎？

(6) 這條河能不能釣魚？

3. Complete the following dialogues with affirmative-negative questions:

(1) A : _____ ?

　　　　　　　(433, 434, 435)

B：他不會作這些練習。

(2) A：＿＿＿＿＿？

　　B：我能幫助你。

(3) A：＿＿＿＿＿？

　　B：我可以教你開車。

(4) A：＿＿＿＿＿？

　　B：他不想研究音樂，他要研究文學。

(5) A：＿＿＿＿＿？

　　B：我要休息休息。

4. Supply "要", "想", "能", "可以", "會" or "應該" in the following sentences:

　　明天我們＿＿去參觀圖書館，我＿＿請我朋友跟我們一起去。我給他打電話，問他＿＿去。他說他很＿＿去，可是他上午有事兒，不＿＿去。我說，這個圖書館很大，很有意思，他＿＿去參觀參觀，以後＿＿去那兒看書。他問我，明天下午去，好嗎？我說，下午去也＿＿。我哥哥＿＿開車，下午我們一起坐車去。我朋友很高興，說："好！"

5. Translate the following into Chinese:
(1) He wants to be a doctor.
(2) Do you want to buy a ticket for the Beijing opera?
(3) He is very good at fishing.
(4) Singing is prohibited in the reading-rooms.
(5) You should take some exercise every day.
(6) He can teach you English.

(7) Can you watch TV tonight?

(8) You can get to know still more.

(9) I intend to make a study of Chinese proverbs.

八、語音語調 Pronunciation and Intonation

1. Sentence tunes (2)

(1) Questions formed with interrogative pronouns are usually said in the high-pitch sentence tune. Interrogative pronouns are usually stressed, and the sentence ends in a fall. E.g.

你想作什麼工作?

——我想當翻譯。

丁雲在作什麼?

——她在游泳呢。

在哪兒停車?

這是誰的車?

(2) Affirmative-negative questions formed with affirmative and negative forms of optative verbs are usually said in the high-pitch sentence tune. The affirmative part is stressed, the negative part is pronounced with a weak stress. The sentence ends in a falling intonation. In answers, the optative verbs should be stressed. E.g.

今年能不能去？

—今年能去。

他會不會說英語？

—他會說英語。

(3) Exclamatory sentences containing the modal particle "啊" are usually said rather slowly and in the low-pitch sentence tune, trailing off to a falling intonation towards the end. E.g.

這很不容易啊！

那很難啊！

2. Exercises

Read out the following poem:

Dēng Guàn Què Lóu
登 鸛 雀 樓

Wáng Zhīhuàn
王 之 渙

Bái   rì   yī   shān   jìn,
白 日 依 山 盡,

Huáng   hé   rù   hǎi   liú.
黃 河 入 海 流。

Yù   qióng   qiānlǐ   mù,
欲 窮 千里 目,

Gèng   shàng   yìcéng   lóu.
更 上 一層 樓。

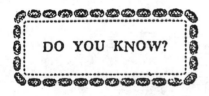

DO YOU KNOW?

Lu Xun and Guo Moruo

Lu Xun and Guo Moruo were both great modern Chinese writers.

Lu Xun was a great man of letters, thinker and revolutionary, as well as the founder of modern Chinese literature. His real name was Chou Shuren, and Lu Xun was his penname. He was born on Sept. 25, 1881 in Shaoxing County, Zhejiang Province and died on October 19, 1936 in Shanghai. His famous novels "A Madman's Diary" and "The True Story of Ah-Q" laid the foundation of modern Chinese literature and revolutionary realism. His works have been collected in the "Complete Works of Lu Xun", totalling 20 volumes.

Guo Moruo was a great proletarian cultural fighter and an outstanding man of letters, revolutionary, scientist, thinker and social activist. He was born on November 16, 1892 in the town of Shawan, Luoshan County, Sichuan Province and died on June 12, 1978 in Beijing at the age of 86. "Goddess", a famous poem of his, filled with revolutionary romanticism, blazed a trail for modern Chinese poetry. After Lu Xun, Guo Moruo was another brilliant banner on China's cultural front. The "Collected Works of Mo Ruo" total 17 volumes.

Hónghú Shuǐ, Làng Dǎ Làng

第二十七課

一、課　文

電影開始了嗎

（在中國大使館）
(Zài Zhōngguó dàshǐguǎn)

王　　：你們都來了，請進！
Wang:　Nǐmen dōu lái le, qǐng jìn!

布　朗：您好！能參加今天的招待會，我非常高興。
Bulang:　Nín hǎo! Néng cānjiā jīntiān de zhāodàihuì, wǒ fēicháng gāoxìng.

古　波：丁雲，電影開始了嗎？
Gubo:　Dīng Yún, diànyǐng kāishǐ le ma?

丁　雲：還沒有開始呢。你們要喝點兒什麼酒？
Ding Yun:　Hái méiyou kāishǐ ne.　Nǐmen yào hē diǎnr shénme jiǔ?

布　朗：我想嘗嘗中國的茅台酒。
Bulang:　Wǒ xiǎng chángchang Zhōngguó de máotáijiǔ.

布朗太太： 我不會喝酒，要一杯橘子水吧。
Bulang Taitai:　Wǒ bú huì hē jiǔ, yào yìbēi júzishuǐ ba.

王　： 為布朗先生和布朗太太的健康乾杯！
Wang:　Wèi Bùlǎng Xiānsheng hé Bùlǎng Tàitai de jiànkāng gān bēi!

布　朗： 謝謝，為我們的友誼乾杯！
Bulang:　Xièxie, wèi wǒmen de yǒuyì gān bēi!

丁　雲： 帕蘭卡，茅台酒你喝了沒有？
Ding Yun:　Pàlánkǎ, máotáijiǔ nǐ hē le méiyou?

帕蘭卡： 沒有。我喝了一杯中國葡萄酒。
Palanka:　Méiyou. Wǒ hē le yìbēi Zhōngguó pútáojiǔ.

丁　雲： 請你們嘗嘗中國菜。
Ding Yun:　Qǐng nǐmen chángchang Zhōngguó cài.

太　太： 謝謝，我吃了。非常好。
Taitai:　Xièxie, wǒ chī le. Fēicháng hǎo.

古　波： 筷子我還用得不好，我想再試一試。
Gubo:　Kuàizi wǒ hái yòng de bù hǎo, wǒ xiǎng zài shìyishi.

王　： 我給你們介紹介紹：這是大使館的文化參贊李先生
Wang:　Wǒ gěi nǐmen jièshaojièshao: Zhè shì dàshǐguǎn de wénhuà cānzàn Lǐ Xiānsheng

和夫人，這是布朗先生和布朗太太。
hé fūren, zhè shì Bùlǎng Xiānsheng hé Bùlǎng Tàitai.

布　朗：認識你們，我很高興。
Bulang:　Rènshi nǐmen, wǒ hěn gāoxìng.

參　贊：歡迎，歡迎。
Canzan:　Huānyíng, huānyíng.

王　：這兩位是中文系的學生，古波和帕蘭卡。他們今年九
Wang:　Zhè liǎngwèi shì Zhōngwén xì de xuésheng, Gǔbō hé Pàlánkǎ. Tāmen jīnnián jiǔyuè

月就要去中國學習。
jiù yào qù Zhōngguó xuéxí.

參　贊：太好了，我們又認識了兩位年輕的朋友。
Canzan:　Tài hǎo le, wǒmen yòu rènshi le liǎngwèi niánqīng de péngyou.

夫　人：請大家到樓上看電影吧。
Furen:　Qǐng dàjiā dào lóushàng kàn diànyǐng ba.

二、生　詞

1. 開始	kāishǐ	to begin, to start
2. 大使館	dàshǐguǎn	embassy
大使	dàshǐ	ambassador
3. 招待會	zhāodàihuì	reception
4. 酒	jiǔ	wine, spirit
5. 嘗	cháng	to taste
6. 茅台酒	máotáijiǔ	Maotai (a Chinese strong liquor)

7.為	wèi	for, to
8.健康	jiànkāng	health, healthy
9.乾杯	gān bēi	to drink a toast, to propose a toast, here's to
10.友誼	yǒuyì	friendship
11.葡萄酒	pútáojiǔ	wine
葡萄	pútáo	grape
12.菜	cài	dish, vegetable
13.筷子	kuàizi	chopsticks
14.試	shì	to try
15.文化	wénhuà	culture
16.參贊	cānzàn	counsellor
17.夫人	fūren	lady, madame, Mrs.
18.又	yòu	again, in addition to, more
19.大家	dàjiā	all, everybody
20.到	dào	to go, to arrive, to reach
21.樓	lóu	storied building, floor

專　名

李	Lǐ	a surname

補　充　詞

1. 白蘭地　　　　báilándì　　　　brandy
2. 香檳酒　　　　xiāngbīnjiǔ　　　champagne
3. 武官　　　　　wǔguān　　　　　military attaché
4. 一秘　　　　　yīmì　　　　　　first secretary
5. 病　　　　　　bìng　　　　　　to fall ill, illness, disease
6. 小學生　　　　xiǎoxuéshēng　　pupil, schoolboy (schoolgirl)

三、閱讀短文

學　寫　字

　　一位老師在教小學生寫字。他寫了一個“一”字，問小學生認識不認識。小學生說：“我認識，這是‘一’字。”

　　老師說：“對，你寫吧。”

　　小學生也寫了一個“一”字，問老師：“您看，我寫得對不對？”

　　“你寫得很好。”老師說，“你會寫‘二’字嗎？”

　　小學生回答得很快：“我會寫，‘一’字是一橫 (héng, horizontal stroke in Chinese characters)，‘二’字是兩橫。”他又寫了一個“二”字。

　　老師說：“對了。‘三’字呢？”

　　　　　　　　　(448, 456, 457)

“‘三’字是三橫。”

老師還想教他寫“四”、“五”……小學生説：“您不用教我，我都會寫。”

老師讓他寫一個“萬 (wàn, ten thousand) ”字。

小學生想：“萬”字一定是一萬橫。他回家準備了十張紙，開始寫“萬”字。

下午上課的時候，老師問他：“你寫的‘萬’字呢？”

小學生回答：“這九張紙都是我寫的‘萬’字，還差八十二橫。”

四、注釋 Notes

1. "能參加今天的招待會，我非常高興。"

   "I'm very glad that I can attend the reception today."

   "認識你們，我很高興"

   "I'm very glad to make your acquaintance."

   "能參加今天的招待會，我非常高興。" and "認識你們，我很高興。" are both compound sentences in which the first clauses tell the reason why the subject "我" is glad. "我" in clauses of this type is more often than not omitted.

2. "為我們的友誼乾杯！"

   "To our friendship!"

   "為⋯乾杯" is an expression used to propose a toast. "為" here is a preposition. The prepositional construction "為⋯" introduced in this lesson tells the purpose of the action expressed by the verb that is used in this construction and is invariably placed before the verb.

3. "我們又認識了兩位年輕的朋友。"

   The adverbs "再" (1) and "又" (1) both indicate the repetition of an action, but they are different in usage: "再" (1) is used to denote an action or a state of affairs which has not been repeated yet while "又" (1) is used when the repetition has already occured.

   他今天去圖書館了，他說明天再去。

   他昨天上午來了，下午沒有再來。

   他昨天來了，今天又來了。

   他昨天沒有來，今天又沒有來。

4. "請大家到樓上看電影吧。"

   "Well, everyone, please go upstairs and see the film."

   The pronoun "大家" refers to all the persons concerned.

"樓上" refers to all the upper part of a building from the first floor up. If the speaker is inside the building, "樓上" can also refer to any storey above the storey where he is. "樓下" refers to the ground floor or any floor below where the speaker is.

五、替換與擴展　Substitution and Extension

㈠

1. 他們來了嗎?
   他們都來了。

你們,	鍛鍊
朋友們,	到
同學們,	走
學生們,	懂
服務員,	休息

2. 電影開始了嗎?
   (電影) 還沒有開始呢。
   電影幾點開始?
   七點一刻開始。

電視	京劇
舞會	文學課
招待會	音樂會*

3. 中國菜你嘗了沒有?
   我沒有嘗。
   你想嘗嗎?
   我想嘗。

麵包,	吃
那個問題,	談
新筆,	試
今天的新聞,	聽
飯,	作
電話,	打
桌子,	整理

4. 你喝了茅台酒沒有?
   我喝了，我喝了一杯茅台酒。
   茅台酒怎麼樣?
   不錯。

葡萄酒	礦泉水
啤酒	白蘭地*
花茶	香檳酒*
橘子水	

5. 他雜誌看得多不多?
   不多。
   他看了幾本雜誌?
   他看了兩本雜誌。

成語（個）,	翻譯
雜誌（本）,	買
朋友（位）,	請
菜（個）,	要
電影票（張）,	給
花兒（束）,	送
同學（個）,	輔導

6. 昨天代表團參觀了什麼地方?
   代表團參觀了<u>那個工廠</u>。

一些圖書館 我們學院 學生城的宿舍樓 中文系和英文系 農村

7. (請大家)為<u>我們</u>
   <u>的友誼</u>乾杯!
   乾杯!

我們兩國人民的友誼 參贊先生和夫人的健康 大使先生和夫人的健康 武官*先生和夫人的健康 朋友們的健康

(二)

1. Welcoming a guest

    A：教授*先生，您來了我們很高興。

    B：能參加你們的招待會，真太好了。

    A：我來給你們介紹介紹:
       這是我們的一秘*和夫人，這是布朗教授*。

    B：認識您很高興。

    C：歡迎，歡迎。

A：請嘗嘗這個菜。`

B：謝謝，來一點兒。非常好。

A：來，為我們的友誼再乾一杯！

B：乾杯！

3. At a bus stop

A：請問，這趟(tàng, *a measure word*) 車可以到日本大使館嗎？

B：可以。你看，車來了。

4. Waiting for somebody

老師：同學們都來了嗎？

學生：還沒有呢。

老師：誰還沒有來？

學生：古波和帕蘭卡沒有來。

　　　啊，古波來了。古波，快，大家都在等你呢。

古波：對不起*，我來得太晚了。

學生：帕蘭卡呢？

古波：她不能來，她病*了。

* * * *

請柬 (qǐngjiǎn, invitation card)

謹訂於一九八〇年十二月二十日星期六晚七點在中
國大使館舉行電影招待會，請出席。
中國大使館文化參贊　李志民

六、語法　Grammar

The perfect aspect of an action

(1)　Particles added to verbs to tell in what stage an action is are called aspect particles.

The perfect aspect of an action is shown by adding the aspect particle "了" to the verb. E.g.

①　他們都來嗎?
　　Are all of them coming?

②　他們都來了嗎?
　　Have they all come?

他們都來。
Yes, they are (all coming).

他們都來了。
Yes, they have (all come).

你看幾本雜誌?
How many copies of magazines are you going to read?

你看了幾本雜誌?
How many copies of magazines have you read?

我看三本雜誌。
I am going to read three (copies of magazines).

我看了三本雜誌。
I have read three (copies of magazines).

The completion of an action only tells in what stage the action itself is and has nothing to do with the time (past, present or future) when it takes place. Very often a completed action took place in the past. Nevertheless, a past action is not always followed by the aspect particle "了". For example, if a past action is a habitual one or when it is a simple statement and there is no need to emphasize its completion, the aspect particle "了" is

(458, 459)

not used. E.g.

以前他常常來看我。

去年 (qùnián, last year) 他在學生宿舍住。

A completed action may take place either in the past or in the future.
E.g.

明天晚上我吃了飯看電影。

(2) When a verb with the aspect particle " 了 " takes after it an object,
the object is usually qualified by a numeral-measure word or other attributive.

Nouns or pronouns	Verbs	" 了 "	Numeral-measure words or pronouns or adjectives	Nouns or pronouns
他 同學們 我 她	認識 訪問 買 回答	了 了 了 了	兩個 那位 新 老師的	朋友。 教練。 地圖。 問題。

The sentence will sometimes sound incomplete when its object is a
simple one and does not have any attributive (e.g. "他看了雜誌" or "代表
團參觀了工廠") and it is necessary to add a number of complementary
elements to make the meaning complete.

(3) The negative form of the perfect aspect of an action is made by
putting the adverb " 沒 (有) " before the verb after which no " 了 " is allowed. E.g.

他們沒有來。

我沒看雜誌。

For an action that is bound to happen or be completed, but has as yet not happened or been completed, the construction "還沒（有）…呢" is used. E.g.

電影還沒（有）開始呢。

他還沒（有）來呢。

To answer questions of this type, either "沒有" or "還沒有呢" may be used to indicate that the action hasn't as yet completed. E.g.

你作了練習沒有?

沒有。

（還沒有呢。）

(4) Affirmative-negative form of the perfect aspect of an action:

The affirmative-negative form of the perfect aspect of an action is usually "…了沒有".

Nouns or pronouns	Verbs	"了"	Nouns or pronouns	"沒有"
電影	開始	了		沒有?
你	喝	了	茅台酒	沒有?
你們	都看	了	今天的報	沒有?

The affirmative-negative form of the perfect aspect of an action can also be made by juxtaposing the affirmative and negative forms of the verb (i.e. " …沒… "), e.g. "來沒來", "喝沒喝".

Nouns or pronouns	Verbs	"沒"	Verbs	Nouns or pronouns
他 你 你們	來 寫 談	沒 沒 沒	來? 寫 談	 信? 這個問題?

七、練習　Exercises

1.　Read out the following phrases:

開始工作　　　　開始學習　　　　開始研究
開始了解　　　　開始訪問　　　　開始參觀
開始跳舞　　　　開始鍛鍊　　　　身體健康
祝你健康　　　　非常健康　　　　不太健康
研究了這本語法　　　　訪問了這位作家
翻譯了他的書　　　　　認識了很多朋友
參加了那個舞會　　　　了解了一些問題
聽了這張唱片　　　　　問了兩個問題
穿了新裙子　　　　　　釣了五條魚
接了不少電話　　　　　看了中國電影

2. Rewrite the following sentences using "了" to indicate the completion of an action:

(1) 我買一本漢語詞典。

(2) 他要兩杯咖啡。

(3) 王老師給我們兩張京劇票。

(4) 今天他們參觀我們的學校。

(5) 他跟我們一起訪問那位有名的作家。

3. Answer the following groups of questions in the negative:

(1) 你哥哥走嗎?

你哥哥走了嗎?

(2) 他姐姐來嗎?

他姐姐來了嗎?

(3) 你們鍛鍊嗎?

你們鍛鍊了嗎?

(4) 古波研究不研究中國音樂?

古波研究沒研究中國音樂?

(5) 他們吃不吃飯?

他們吃飯了沒有?

(6) 你了解不了解那個問題?

你了解沒了解那個問題?

4. Make sentences using the following words and phrases in the same way as the example given:

Example 喝 葡萄酒

→你們喝了葡萄酒沒有?

我喝了兩杯，他沒喝。

(1) 買　　電影票

(2) 寫　　漢字

(3) 參觀　工廠

(4) 問　　問題

(5) 學習　生詞

(6) 訪問　作家

5. Change the following to affirmative-negative questions:

(1) 我們懂了。

(2) 她試了中國筷子。

(3) 我們都參加了大使館的招待會。

(4) 他看了這個電影。

(5) 我用了那本詞典。

(6) 我們談了那個問題。

6. Supply "再" or "又" in the following sentences:

(1) 他復習了今天的課文，＿＿＿復習了昨天的課文。

(2) 這個商店的麵包很好，我買了兩個，下午我想＿＿＿買兩個。

(3) 古波下午給帕蘭卡打了電話，晚上＿＿＿給她打了電話。

(4) 這本小說很好，我要＿＿＿看看。

(5) 那個電影我看了，今天不想＿＿＿看。

(6) 他星期二沒有上課，今天＿＿＿沒有上課。

7. Retell the Reading Text with the help of the following pictures:

八、語音語調 **Pronunciation and Intonation**

1. Sentence tunes (3)

Affirmative-negative questions built on the pattern "…了沒有" are usually uttered in a rather high pitch. "沒有" is pronounced with a weak stress and the sentence ends in a falling intonation. E.g.

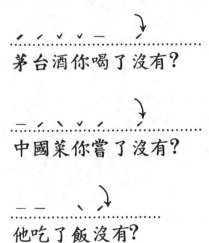

茅台酒你喝了沒有？

中國菜你嘗了沒有？

他吃了飯沒有？

2. Exercises

Read out the following words or phrases containing c and ch, paying special attention to the pronunciation of these two sounds:

詞—吃   詞典—吃飯

吃菜—生詞

層—成　　千層—成語

三層—長城

Read out the following proverbs:

Chā　yǐ　háo　lí,

差　以　毫　厘，

shī　zhī　qiānlǐ.

失　之　千里。

(A minimal error or deviation results in wide divergence.)

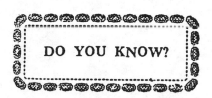

DO YOU KNOW?

The Chinese Strong Drink—Mao Tai

Mao Tai is a famous alcoholic drink, produced in China in the town of Maotai, Renhuai County, Guizhou Province. It ranks first in China's eight famous drinks. It is of an exquisite flavour, transparent and clear like crystal. Containing 53 percent alcohol, it nevertheless tastes mild and mellow, not going to the head. Maotai enjoys a high reputation throughout the world.

Among China's famous traditional alcoholic drinks are also Fen Wine of Shanxi Province, Daqu Wine of Sichuan Province and Shaoxing Wine of Zhejiang Province.

第二十八課

一、課 文

我去看足球賽了

帕蘭卡：古波，昨天上午我給你打電話了，你不在。你去

Palanka: Gǔbō, zuótiān shàngwǔ wǒ gěi nǐ dǎ diànhuà le, nǐ bú zài. Nǐ qù

哪兒了？

nǎr le?

古　波：我去中國大使館辦簽證了。

Gubo: Wǒ qù Zhōngguó dàshǐguǎn bàn qiānzhèng le.

帕蘭卡：下午呢？你又不在。

Palanka: Xiàwǔ ne? Nǐ yòu bú zài.

古　波：我吃了午飯就去看足球賽了。

Gubo: Wǒ chī le wǔfàn jiù qù kàn zúqiú sài le.

帕蘭卡：誰跟誰賽？

Palanka: Shéi gēn shéi sài?

古　波：大學生隊跟銀行隊賽。
Gubo:　Dàxuéshēng duì gēn yínháng duì sài.

帕蘭卡：大學生隊贏他們了嗎？
Palanka:　Dàxuéshēng duì yíng tāmen le ma?

古　波：沒有，大學生隊輸了，一比二。裁判不公平。
Gubo:　Méiyou, dàxuéshēng duì shū le, yī bǐ èr. Cáipàn bù gōngpíng.

帕蘭卡：你總說裁判不公平。
Palanka:　Nǐ zǒng shuō cáipàn bù gōngpíng.

古　波：你沒去看，昨天大學生隊踢得很好。真氣人。
Gubo:　Nǐ méi qù kàn, zuótiān dàxuéshēng duì tī de hěn hǎo. Zhēn qì rén.

帕蘭卡：好了，我問你，你的行李準備得怎麼樣？
Palanka:　Hǎo le, wǒ wèn nǐ, nǐ de xíngli zhǔnbèi de zěnmeyàng?

古　波：我正整理箱子呢。我還差一頂帽子。你呢？
Gubo:　Wǒ zhèng zhěnglǐ xiāngzi ne. Wǒ hái chà yìdǐng màozi. Nǐ ne?

帕蘭卡：我想買一雙冰鞋。北京冬天可以滑冰。
Palanka:　Wǒ xiǎng mǎi yìshuāng bīngxié. Běijīng dōngtiān kěyǐ huá bīng.

古　波：我送你一雙冰鞋吧。
Gubo:　Wǒ sòng nǐ yìshuāng bīngxié ba.

帕蘭卡：非常感謝。我給你買帽子，好嗎？
Palanka:　Fēicháng gǎnxiè. Wǒ gěi nǐ mǎi màozi, hǎo ma?

古　波：我也要謝謝你。明天吃了早飯我們就去商店。

Gubo: Wǒ yě yào xièxie nǐ. Míngtiān chī le zǎofàn wǒmen jiù qù shāngdiàn.

二、生　詞

1.足球	zúqiú	football
球	qiú	ball
2.賽	sài	to compete, competition, match
3.昨天	zuótiān	yesterday
4.辦	bàn	to do, to handle, to attend to, to tackle
5.簽證	qiānzhèng	visa
6.午飯	wǔfàn	lunch
7.隊	duì	team
8.贏	yíng	to win, to beat
9.輸	shū	to lose
10.比	bǐ	a preposition showing comparison, than, to
11.裁判	cáipàn	referee, umpire, to act as a referee, to judge
12公平	gōngpíng	fair
13.踢	tī	to kick
14.氣人	qìrén	to get someone angry, to get someone annoyed

(475, 476)

15.行李	xíngli	luggage, baggage
16.箱子	xiāngzi	suitcase
17.頂	dǐng	a measure word
18.帽子	màozi	hat, cap
19.雙	shuāng	a measure word, pair
20.冰鞋	bīngxié	skating boots, skates
鞋	xié	shoes
21.冬天	dōngtiān	winter
22.滑冰	huá bīng	to skate, skating
23.早飯	zǎofàn	breakfast

補 充 詞

1.體育場	tǐyùchǎng	stadium
2.公園	gōngyuán	park
3.乒乓球	pīngpāngqiú	table tennis
4.運動	yùndòng	sports, to do exercise
5.網球	wǎngqiú	tennis
6.籃球	lánqiú	basketball
7.排球	páiqiú	volleyball
8.滑雪	huá xuě	to ski, skiing

三、閱讀短文

看 足 球 賽

今天是八月二十七號，星期四。下午帕蘭卡來找我，我不在，我去看足球賽了。

上午我去中國大使館辦了簽證就回宿舍了。吃午飯的時候，我的朋友比里問我：" 古波，一點半體育場有足球賽，你想去看嗎？" 他知道我很喜歡看足球賽，以前體育場有足球賽的時候，我們總是一起去看。我說：" 我很想去，可是我正準備行李呢，沒有空兒去買票。" 他說：" 我哥哥給了我兩張票，我們一起去吧！" 我說：" 太好了，謝謝你。"

吃了午飯，我們就坐車去體育場了。我們到了那兒的時候，很多人正在外邊等票呢。我們從東邊的門進體育場。五分鐘以後，比賽就開始了。

今天大學生隊跟銀行隊賽，這是兩個有名的足球隊。比里問我：" 你說今天哪個隊能贏？" 我說：" 大學生隊一定贏。" 他說：" 不一定。我想銀行隊能贏。"

這兩個隊都踢得很好。今天，大學生隊踢得更好，兩點三刻，他們進了一個球。這個球踢得很漂亮。我說：" 比里，怎麼樣？大學生隊能贏吧？" 比里沒有回答。忽然(hūrán, suddenly)他說：" 好球！銀行隊進了一個球！"

這時候，兩個隊是一比一。十分鐘以後，大學生隊又進了一個球，可是裁判説這個球不算(suàn, to count)　。還有三分鐘了，銀行隊又進了一個球。

二比一，大學生隊輸了，真氣人！

四、注釋 Notes

1. "我吃了午飯就去看足球賽了。"

"I went to see the football match right after lunch."

"明天吃了早飯我們就去商店。"

"We shall go to the shop right after breakfast tomorrow."

To indicate that two actions take place one immediately after the other, that is, the second action is to take place just after the completion of the first one, the aspect particle "了" must be added to the verb indicating the first action and the adverb "就" (2) is usually used before the verb indicating the second action.

2. "一比二。"

"1 : 2" as a record of points gained in sport is read as "一比二". "幾比幾" is an expression used to ask what the score is.

五、替換與擴展 Substitution and Extension

(一)

1. 上午你去哪兒了?

我去中國大使館了。

回,	家
進,	城
去,	城外玩兒
去,	公園 *
去,	體育場 *

2. 昨天晚上你看電影了沒有?

沒有。我看足球賽了。

你看足球賽的時候，你朋友作什麼呢？
他復習課文呢。

聽新聞，	看電視
去咖啡館，	看朋友
看京劇，	準備行李
跳舞，	打乒乓球 *

3. 你買沒買冰鞋？
我沒買（冰鞋）。

吃，	午飯
嘗，	魚湯
辦，	簽證
去，	樓上
當，	裁判

4. 昨天他下了課作什麼了？
昨天他下了課就去滑冰了。

吃，	早飯，	去買箱子
參觀，	工廠，	去接朋友
歡迎，	代表團，	參加招待會
看，	電影，	去打網球 *
買，	帽子，	去看籃球 * 賽

5. 明天你吃了午飯去哪兒？
   明天我吃了午飯就進城。
   我想跟你一起去，好嗎？
   好，我們一起去。

吃，	早飯，	去大使館
下，	課，	去工廠
吃，	晚飯，	去王老師家
看，	排球 * 賽，	去古波那兒

6. 大學生隊贏他們了嗎？
   沒有，大學生隊輸了。
   大學生隊踢得怎麼樣？
   踢得不太好。

工人隊
留學生代表隊
你們隊
北京隊
男隊

(二)

1. Confirming that something has already taken place

   A：星期天你休息得怎麼樣？

   B：我們一家人都去公園 * 了。

   A：你們玩兒得很好吧？

   B：玩兒得不錯。你作什麼了？

A：下午我去商店了。

B：你買沒買東西?

A：我給孩子買了一雙冰鞋和一個小足球。

           *   *   *

A：昨天你去哪兒了? 我下午到宿舍找你了，你不在。

B：我去看朋友了。真對不起 *。

A：沒關係 *，我沒有給你打電話，你不知道我要來。

B：你在宿舍等我了嗎?

A：沒有，我留 (liú, to leave) 了一個條子 (tiáozi, note)
　　就走了。

2. Talking about sports

　　A：你打籃球 * 了嗎?

　　B：沒有，我踢足球了。

　　A：你每天都鍛錬嗎?

　　B：是啊。你喜歡什麼運動?

　　A：我喜歡打網球 *，也常常
　　　　打乒乓球 *。冬天我喜歡滑雪 *。

　　B：我不太會滑雪 *，今年冬天你教我，好嗎?

　　A：可以，我也滑得不太好。

           *   *   *

六、語法 **Grammar**

Modal particle "了" (1)

1. Apart from indicating aspect, "了" may also function as a modal particle employed to denote the attitude of speaker. As an aspect particle, "了" usually comes after the verb, but it is always found at the end of the sentence when serving as a modal particle. The modal particle "了" may be used to express various different shades of meaning. "了" introduced in this lesson (Use 1) is used to modify the whole sentence to indicate that the event referred to has already taken place. Compare these two dialogues:

① 你去哪兒?

Where are you going?

我去商店。

I'm going to the shop.

② 你去哪兒了?

Where have you been? (or Where did you go?)

我去商店了。

I have been to the shop. (or I went to the shop.)

你買什麼?

What are you going
to buy?

我買麵包。

I'm going to buy some
bread.

你買什麼了?

What have you bought? (or
What did you buy?)

我買麵包了。

I have bought some bread.
(or I bought some bread.)

In the first dialogue, "去商店" and "買麵包" are represented as not having taken place as yet; in the second dialogue, they are represented as already accomplished.

The modal particle "了" (1) is usually used to indicate that the action or event referred to is something that took place at some time in the past, but past happenings are not always indicated with the help of the modal particle "了". It is not used, for instance, in simple statements of certain events, especially a succession of events in the past, nor is "了" used in mere description of the background against which something took place, that is, there is no need to stress the completion of what happened. E.g.

昨天他上午去中國大使館，下午去看足球賽。

我去看他的時候，他在家休息呢。

2. The negative form of the sentence with the modal particle "了" is also made by putting the adverb "沒(有)" in front of the verb and at the same time dropping the "了" at the end of the sentence. The affirmative-negative form of such a sentence is made by either adding "…了沒有" at the end of the sentence or by juxtaposing the affirmative and negative forms of the verb, (i.e. "…沒… ").

Nouns or pronouns	Adverb	Verbs	Nouns or pronouns	Particles
我 他 妹妹 你	沒（有）	看 買 吃 吃沒吃	電影 冰鞋。 午飯 午飯？	了。 了沒有？

3. When " 了 " comes after the verb and at the end of the sentence as well, it functions both as an aspect particle and a modal particle. E.g.

他來了。

我們懂了。

學生隊贏了。

七、練習 Exercises

1. Read out the following phrases:

昨天上午　昨天下午　昨天晚上

今天上午　今天下午　今天晚上

明天上午　明天下午　明天晚上

吃早飯　吃午飯　吃晚飯　吃點心　　吃菜

打電話　打乒乓球　打籃球　打網球　打球

看球賽　看電視　看電影　看京劇　看信

看雜誌　看報　看書　看照片　看畫報

聽音樂　聽民歌　聽唱片　聽新聞

作練習　作飯　　作菜　　作點心　作裙子

2. Change the following to affirmative-negative questions:

    (1) 昨天下午我看足球賽了。

    (2) 代表團到北京了。

    (3) 她跟丁雲打乒乓球了。

    (4) 古波辦簽證了。

    (5) 大學生隊贏工人隊了。

    (6) 他當裁判了。

    (7) 我朋友參加昨天晚上的舞會了。

    (8) 王老師請布朗先生和布朗太太了。

    (9) 他們研究這個問題了。

    (10) 我們都喝咖啡了。

3. Complete the following dialogues:

    (1) A：昨天下午你去看比里了沒有?

       B：＿＿＿＿＿＿＿＿＿＿。

       A：他在宿舍作什麼了?

       B：＿＿＿＿＿＿＿＿＿＿。

    (2) A：＿＿＿＿＿＿＿＿＿＿?

       B：星期日我們去城外玩兒了。

       A：丁雲去沒去?

       B：＿＿＿＿＿＿＿＿＿＿。

    (3) A：你參觀農村了沒有?

       B：＿＿＿＿＿＿＿＿＿＿。

(488, 489)

A：你訪問沒訪問農民？

B：＿＿＿＿＿＿＿＿＿ 。

(4) A：你接電話了嗎？

B：＿＿＿＿＿＿＿＿＿ 。

A：＿＿＿＿＿＿＿＿＿ ？

B：我同學給我打電話了。

(5) A：今天下午你去商店了沒有？

B：＿＿＿＿＿＿＿＿＿ 。

A：＿＿＿＿＿＿＿＿＿ ？

B：我在商店買了一雙鞋。

(6) A：＿＿＿＿＿＿＿＿＿ ？

B：我沒有給他們買足球票。

A：＿＿＿＿＿＿＿＿＿ ？

B：他們都不去看足球賽。

4. Make sentences after the example with the words and phrases given, using "了" and the adverb "就" to show that two actions follow closely one after another:

Example

吃午飯

滑冰

→我吃了午飯就去滑冰了。

(1) 到工廠　　　　　(2) 復習課文

　　開始參觀　　　　　　寫漢字

(3) 下課　　　　　　(4) 作練習

寫信   看電視

(5) 聽今天的新聞

睡覺

5. Answer the following questions on the Reading Text:

(1) 上午古波作什麼了？

(2) 誰給古波足球賽的票了？

(3) 今天誰跟誰賽？

(4) 古波想哪個隊能贏？

(5) 這兩個隊踢得怎麼樣？

(6) 哪個隊贏了？

6. Write a short passage according to what the following eight pictures indicate.

他昨天作什麼了？

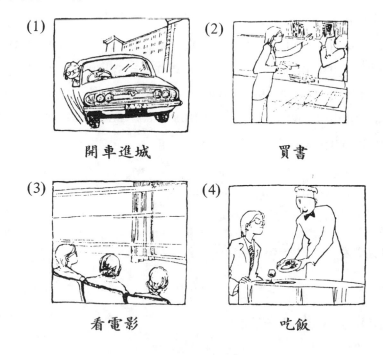

(1) 開車進城

(2) 買書

(3) 看電影

(4) 吃飯

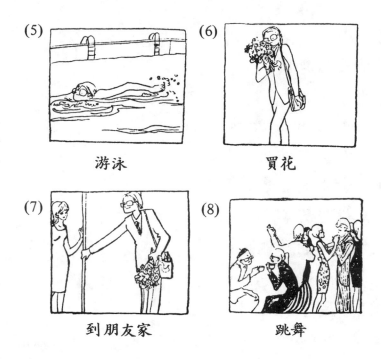

(5) 游泳

(6) 買花

(7) 到朋友家

(8) 跳舞

八、語音練習　**Pronunciation and Intonation**

1.　Sentence tunes (4)

(1)　In simple questions formed with the modal particle "呢", if a monosyllabic word precedes "呢", the monosyllabic word is stressed, with the voice drawing out a bit towards the end and the pitch slightly lower. This word, together with "呢", forms a sentence uttered in the high-pitch sentence tune with a fall at the end. E.g.

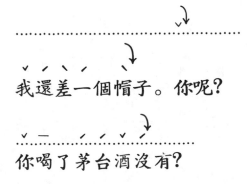

我還差一個帽子。你呢?

你喝了茅台酒沒有?

——我喝了。你呢?

你来了。他呢?

(2) The sentence tune for this type of questions can be divided at the word "好" into two parts. The first part or the part before "好" is uttered in the low-pitch sentence tune, but the voice does not fall but rises slightly at the end. A short pause comes before "好". The word "好" is stressed with the voice drawing out a bit. The word "好", together with "嗎", forms the second part uttered in the high-pitch sentence tune with a rise at the end. E.g.

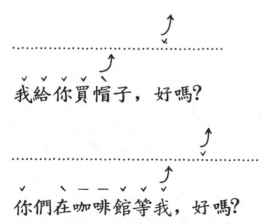

我給你買帽子,好嗎?

你們在咖啡館等我,好嗎?

2. Continuous changes of tones of three or more than three 3rd tone syllables

(1) When three words in the 3rd tone come together in close succession, the first two words usually change to the 2nd tone with the third one retaining the 3rd tone (or changing to the half 3rd tone). When the first

word is emphasized or when it is followed by a pause, then it is pronounced in the half third-tone. E.g.

你好嗎?

我很好，你呢?

（"我"、"很"讀第二聲，"好"讀半三聲。"）

也很好　　（"也"、"很"讀第二聲。）

(2)　Wore than three words in the 3rd tone come together in close succession, they can be divided into tone-groups (marked with a slant stroke "/" in this book) according to their grammatical relationships. Each tone-group may consist of one, two or three syllables and is pronounced according to the rules concerning changes of words in the 3rd tone. For words following closely on one another, the first or the first two words are pronounced in the 2nd tone. Words followed by a slight pause are pronounced in the half 3rd tone. E.g.

我給你 / 買帽子。

（"我"、"給"讀第二聲，"你"、"買"讀半三聲。）

我 / 也想買 / 一雙冰鞋。

（"我"讀半三聲，"也"、"想"讀第二聲，"買"讀半三聲。）

第二十九課

一、課 文

飛 機 就 要 起 飛 了

（在機場）
(Zài jīchǎng)

古　波：你看，同學們都來了，王老師和丁雲也來了。
Gubo:　Nǐ kàn, tóngxuémen dōu lái le, Wáng Lǎoshī hé Dīng Yún yě lái le.

帕蘭卡：丁雲，我們快要分別了，我真不願意離開你。
Palanka:　Dīng Yún, wǒmen kuài yào fēnbié le, wǒ zhēn bú yúanyì líkāi nǐ.

丁　雲：帕蘭卡，我也不願意離開你。我想我們很快會在中國
Ding Yun:　Pàlánkǎ, wǒ yě bú yúanyì líkāi nǐ. Wǒ xiǎng wǒmen hěn kuài huì zài Zhōngguó

　　　　見面。
　　　　jiàn miàn.

古　波：王老師，我們非常感謝您。
Gubo:　Wáng Lǎoshī, wǒmen fēicháng gǎnxiè nín.

布　朗：我太太和我也要謝謝您。您工作非常認真，教得很好，
Bulang:　Wǒ tàitai hé wǒ yě yào xièxie nín. Nín gōngzuò fēicháng rènzhēn, jiāo de hěn hǎo,

　　　　所以他們進步很快。
　　　　suǒyǐ tāmen jìnbù hěn kuài.

王　：哪裏，這是我應該作的。他們學習都很努力，所以能
Wang:　Nǎli, zhè shǐ wǒ yīnggāi zuò de. Tāmen xuéxí dōu hěn nǔlì, suǒyǐ néng

　　　　學得很好。
　　　　xué de hěn hǎo.

帕蘭卡：爸爸要給我們照相了。
Palanka:　Bàba yào gěi wǒmen zhàoxiàng le.

布　朗：請大家站得緊一點兒！好。古波，你們準備準備就上
Bulang:　Qǐng dàjiā zhàn de jǐn yìdiǎnr! Hǎo. Gǔbō, nǐmen zhǔnbeizhǔnbei jiù shàng

　　　　飛機吧。
　　　　fēijī ba.

太　太：帕蘭卡，你們要注意身體。
Taitai:　Pàlánkǎ, nǐmen yào zhùyì shēnti.

帕蘭卡：媽媽您放心，我們身體都很好。
Palanka:　Māma, nín fàng xīn, wǒmen shēnti dōu hěn hǎo.

太　太：你們到了北京就給我來信。別忘了，一定要來信。
Taitai:　Nǐmen dào le Běijīng jiù gěi wǒ lái xìn. Bié wàng le, yídìng yào lái xìn.

布　朗：好了，別難過了。明年我們去中國看他們。
Bulang:　Hǎo le, bié nánguò le. Míngnián wǒmen qù Zhōngguó kàn tāmen.

古　波：你們明年什麼時候去北京？我們一定到機場接你們。
Gubo:　Nǐmen míngnián shénme shíhou qù Běijīng? Wǒmen yídìng dào jīchǎng jiē nǐmen.

布　朗：明年夏天或者秋天去。飛機就要起飛了，你們快走吧。
Bulang:　Míngnián xiàtiān huòzhě qiūtiān qù. Fēijī jiù yào qǐfēi le, nǐmen kuài zǒu ba.

王　：祝你們身體好，學習好！
Wang:　Zhù nǐmen shēntǐ hǎo, xuéxí hǎo!

丁　雲：祝你們一路平安！
Ding Yun:　Zhù nǐmen yílùpíng'ān!

帕蘭卡、古波：謝謝大家。再見！
Palanka, Gubo:　Xièxie dàjiā. Zàijiàn!

二、生　詞

1. 飛機　　　fēijī　　　　　aeroplane, plane, aircraft

2. 要　　　　yào　　　　　will, to be going to

3. 起飛　　　qǐfēi　　　　　to take off

4. 機場　　　jīchǎng　　　　airfield, airport

5. 分別　　　fēnbié　　　　to part

6. 願意　　　yuànyì　　　　to be willing

7. 離開　　　líkāi　　　　　to leave

8. 見面	jiàn miàn	to meet (see) each other
見	jiàn	to meet, to see
9. 所以	suǒyǐ	so, therefore, as a result
10. 進步	jìnbù	progress, advance, to progress, to make progress
11. 努力	nǔlì	hard-working, studious
12. 照相	zhào xiàng	to take a picture, to have one's photo taken
13. 站	zhàn	to stand
14. 緊	jǐn	close, tight, taut
15. 上	shàng	to get on, to get into, to board
16. 注意	zhùyì	to pay attention to
17. 身體	shēntǐ	body, health
18. 放心	fàng xīn	to set one's mind at rest, to be at ease, to rest assured
19. 忘	wàng	to forget
20. 難過	nánguò	sad
21. 明年	míngnián	next year
22. 夏天	xiàtiān	summer
23. 秋天	qiūtiān	autumn

| 24.一路平安 | yílùpíng'ān | to have a pleasant journey, to have a good trip, bon voyage |

補 充 詞

1.汽車	qìchē	car
2.船	chuán	ship
3.叫	jiào	to hire, to call (a taxi etc.)
4.送行	sòngxíng	to see someone off
5.旅行	lǚxíng	to travel, to tour
6.中國民航	Zhōngguó Mínháng	General Administration of Civil Aviation of China (CAAC)

三、閱讀短文

在 中 國 民 航 的 飛 機 上

"女士 (nǚshì, lady) 們，先生們，你們好！您乘坐 (chéngzuò, to sit) 的是中國民航開往 (kāi wǎng, to leave for) 北京的班機 (bānjī, airliner)。飛機就要起飛了，請大家坐好 (zuòhǎo, to take one's seat)，請不要吸煙……"

廣播 (guǎngbō, broadcast) 裏，漢語說得很清楚，古波和帕蘭卡都懂了，他們非常高興。

飛機上人真多，很多人都是去中國的。兩個穿得很漂亮的中國姑娘請大家吃糖 (táng, sweets)、喝茶，她們是飛機上的服務員。

　　服務員都很年輕，工作非常認真。她們會說英語和法語。古波、帕蘭卡跟她們說漢語，她們很高興。

　　快十二點了，服務員說：“請大家注意，就要吃午飯了。”午飯有麵包和點心，還有四個中國菜。菜作得很好，古波和帕蘭卡都很喜歡吃。

　　帕蘭卡吃了飯想喝咖啡。服務員問古波要咖啡還是要茶。古波說：“我們快要到中國了，我要喝中國茶。”服務員給了他們一杯花茶、一杯咖啡，說：“你們漢語說得真流利。”帕蘭卡說：“哪裏，我們說得不太好。我們倆都是去中國學習的留學生。”

　　服務員說：“歡迎你們到中國學習。”

飛機就要起飛了

四、注釋 Notes

1. "我真不願意離開你。"

"願意" is also an optative verb, indicating that one is willing or agrees to do something, or wishes something good would happen.

2. "我想我們很快會在中國見面。"

"I think we'll soon see each other in China."

The optative verb "會" also indicates probability besides ability acquired or mastered as a result of study. E.g.

他還沒有來。今天他會來嗎？

他不會來。

3. "您工作非常認真，教得很好，所以他們進步很快。"

"所以" is a conjunction showing cause and effect. It usually occurs in the second clause of a compound sentence to tell result.

4. "這是我應該作的。"

"這是我應該作的" is a polite expression used in reply to the praise someone sings of one for what he has done.

5. "請大家站得緊一點兒！"

"Please stand a bit closer, (you all.)"

When used after adjectives or some verbs, "一點兒" implies comparison and indicates that the difference is very slight, e.g. "快一點兒", "早一點兒", "好一點兒" etc.

6. "你們要注意身體。"

"You must take care of yourself."

As well as indicating wish and request, the optative verb "要" can also indicate necessity. Its negative form is "不用". E.g.

這個練習要作嗎？

這個練習不用作。

7. "你們到了北京就給我來信。"

"來信" is a colloquialism, meaning the same as "寫信".

8. "祝你們一路平安!"

"一路平安" means "Have a pleasant journey," "Have a good trip" or "Bon voyage". It is used when one sees somebody off or says good-bye to somebody on departure.

五、替換與擴展　Substitution and Extension

(一)

1. 飛機就要起飛了嗎?
   飛機就要起飛了。快上吧。

火車,	開
汽車*,	開
船*,	開

2. 代表團什麼時候來?
   快要來了。

球賽,	開始
你們,	鍛鍊
飛機,	到
(汽)車,	來

3. 現在幾點?
   七點五十。
   要上課了，請快一點兒。

9：45，	下課
2：30，	比賽
11：55，	吃飯
7：05，	開車
8：15，	照相

4. 別難過了。

忘	找
說	走
玩兒	喝酒

5. 昨天你去看張大明了嗎?
   我去看他了。
   他工作怎麼樣?
   他工作很忙。

學習，	努力
身體，	好
工作，	認真
身體，	健康

(509, 510)

6. 請大家站得緊一點兒。

早　快　慢　好　早

來，走，說，翻譯，起，

(二)

1. Meeting a friend at the airport

A：請問，從北京來的飛機到了沒有?

B：快要到了，還有五分鐘。

A：謝謝。

*　　　*　　　*

A：啊，李先生，您來了。

B：你們好! 謝謝你們來接我。

A：你的行李都到了嗎?

B：還差一個箱子。

A：你在這兒等一等，我去叫＊車。

B：太感謝你了。

2. Seeing someone off

A：火車兩點十分就要開了，請上車吧。

B：謝謝你，再見。

A：你到了那兒就給我來信。

B：好，一定給你寫信。

(510, 511)

A：祝你一路平安，再見！

B：再見！

3. Traveling

A：我快要去中國旅行* 了。

B：你什麼時候走？

A：這個星期六就走。

B：你坐火車去還是坐飛機去？

A：我參加了一個旅行* 團，我們坐中國民航* 的飛機去。

B：你們旅行* 團有多少人？

A：有二十二個。

B：真不少。明年我也想去中國看看。

A：對。你教中國文學，應該去看看。

4. Buying plane tickets

A：先生，我要買兩張去北京的飛機票。

B：你要哪一天的？

A：我要四月十二日中國民航* 612次(cì, No., number)的，還有票嗎？

B：還有。

A：請問飛機什麼時候起飛？

B：上午七點十分。

A：謝謝你。

(511, 512)

六、語法 Grammar

1. "要…了" indicating an action is going to take place in a short time
If we want to indicate that an action or a situation is going to take place soon, we can put the adverb "要" in front of the verb (or adjective) and the modal particle "了" at the end of the sentence to form the construction "要…了". When preceded by "就" or "快" as an adverbial adjunct, "要" shows the imminence. E.g.

爸爸要給我們照相了。

飛機就要起飛了。

我們快要分別了。

Sentences of this kind are turned into questions by having "嗎" added to them at the end. The negative adverb "沒有" is used to form negative answers. E.g.

飛機要起飛了嗎?

沒有。

Points to be noted:

(1) "就要…了" may be preceded by an adverbial of time, as in "他們明天就要走了"; "快要…了" cannot be used in this way.

(2) "要…了" can be changed to "快…了" with its meaning unchanged, e.g. "車快開了".

2. Modal particle "了" (2)

When combined with the negative word "別" or "不要", the modal particle "了" can be used in imperative sentences to indicate that one asks someone to or not to do something. E.g.

別忘了，一定要常來信。

別難過了。

別說了，大家在看書呢。

別找了，你的帽子在這兒。

3. Sentences with a subject-predicate construction as its predicate

A sentence in which a subject-predicate construction serves as the main element of its predicate is known as a sentence with a subject-predicate construction as its predicate. In a great number of sentences of this kind, the person or thing indicated by the subject of the subject-predicate construction is closely related to or forms a component part of the person or thing indicated by the subject of the whole sentence. E.g.

你身體好嗎?

他工作怎麼樣?

七、練習　Exercises

1. Read out the following phrases:

坐飛機　　坐火車　坐汽車 *　　坐船 *

離開朋友　離開家　離開圖書館

離開中國

跟朋友分別　　分別以後　分別的時候

忘了那個生詞　忘了他的名字　忘了來

忘了吃飯

願意去　願意參加　願意了解　願意聽音樂

注意身體　注意學習　注意鍛鍊

請（大家）注意

請放心　您放心　不放心　很放心

2. Complete the following dialogues with "就要...了":

(1) A：今天的報什麼時候來?

B：＿＿＿＿＿＿＿＿＿＿。

(2) A：電影開始了沒有?

B：沒有，＿＿＿＿＿＿＿＿＿＿。

(3) A：我們＿＿＿＿＿＿＿＿＿＿。

B：我真不願意你離開我。

(4) A：車＿＿＿＿＿＿＿＿＿＿，我該走了。

B：祝你一路平安! 再見!

(5) A：他們＿＿＿＿＿＿＿＿＿＿。

B：我們快去歡迎他們。

3. Write dialogues using the following groups of words and phrases in the same way as the example given:

Example　飛機　起飛　十點　差五分十點

→A：飛機幾點起飛?

B：十點起飛。

A：現在幾點?

B：差五分十點。

A：飛機就要起飛了。

(1) 飛機　到　八點　七點五十

(2) 火車　到　九點半　九點二十五

(3) 船　　開　四點一刻　四點十分

(4) 代表團　來　五號　三號

(5) 比賽　開始　星期三　星期二

4. Supply "別…了" in the following sentences:

(1) A：昨天我忘了，我沒有去上課。

B：＿＿＿＿＿＿＿＿，你明天上午九點半還有課。

(2) A：你們就要走了，我很難過。

B：＿＿＿＿＿＿＿＿，以後我們常給你寫信。

(3) A：我們再跳一個舞，好嗎?

B：＿＿＿＿＿＿＿＿，大家都休息了。

(4) A：我在找我的鞋呢。

B：＿＿＿＿＿＿＿＿，你的鞋在這兒。

(5) A：我們再玩兒玩兒吧?

B：＿＿＿＿＿＿＿＿，他們在等我們呢。

5. Translate the following into Chinese, but use sentences with subject-predicate constructions as their predicates:

(1) How are your father and mother?

(2) Is that man a good referee?

(3) There are not many foreign students studying in our institute.

(4) The kitchen in her house is very small, but the dining-hall is quite big.

(5) Are the shirts in this shop good or not?

6. Answer the following questions on the Reading Text:

(1) 古波和帕蘭卡坐的是什麼飛機?

(2) 飛機要起飛了，服務員請大家注意什麼?

(3) 廣播裏漢語說得清楚 * 不清楚? 古波和帕蘭卡懂了沒有?

(4) 飛機上的服務員怎麼樣？

(5) 他們什麼時候吃午飯？午飯怎麼樣？

(6) 古波、帕蘭卡跟服務員説漢語了沒有？他們説了些什麼？

7. Study the picture and answer the following questions, then write a short passage on the picture:

(1) 王英和她愛人去哪兒？

(2) 誰來給他們送行了？

(3) 火車快要開了嗎？

(4) 分別的時候，她們怎麼樣？

(5) 她們在説什麼？

八、語音練習 Pronunciation and Intonation

1. Sentence tunes (5)

(1) In alternative questions the two groups of words indicating the choice are stressed, the connective "還是" is pronounced with a weak stress. The whole sentence can be divided up into two parts. The part before "還是" is uttered in the high-pitch sentence tune, with a rise at the end, and a short pause. The part after "還是" is uttered in the low-pitch sentence tune, with a fall at the end. E.g.

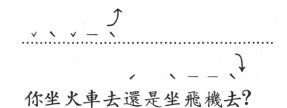

你坐火車去還是坐飛機去？

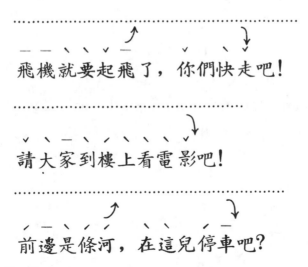

你要咖啡還是要紅茶？

他是學生還是老師？

丁雲想當翻譯還是想當老師？

(2) Imperative sentences or questions formed with the modal particle "吧," are generally said slowly and in the low-pitch sentence tune, and with the voice falling slowly at the end. E.g.

飛機就要起飛了，你們快走吧！

請大家到樓上看電影吧！

前邊是條河，在這兒停車吧？

2. Exercises

(1) Pronounce the following, taking care to differentiate the initials z and zh:

漢字—地址　　知道—雜誌

足球—祝賀　　早飯—招待

作家—桌子　　洗澡—照相

(2) Read out the following trisyllabic words, paying attention to word stress:

不敢當　乒乓球　茅台酒　葡萄酒

礦泉水　橘子水　服務員　星期日

閱覽室　大使館　圖書館　咖啡館

Read out the following proverb:

Zhòng	guā	dé	guā,
種	瓜	得	瓜，
zhòng	dòu	dé	dòu.
種	豆	得	豆。

(Plant melons and you get melons, sow beans and you get beans—as you sow, so will you reap.)

第三十課

復 習

一、課 文

布朗太太笑了

帕蘭卡走了，布朗太太心裏很難過。她請丁雲坐她的車，
Pàlánkǎ zǒu le, Bùlǎng Tàitai xīnli hěn nánguò. Tā qǐng Dīng Yún zuò tā de chē,

她要送丁雲回學生宿舍。
tā yào sòng Dīng Yún huí xuésheng sùshè.

在車上，丁雲說：" 帕蘭卡很想去中國學習，她今天晚上
Zài chēshang, Dīng Yún shuō: "Pàlánkǎ hěn xiǎng qù Zhōngguó xuéxí, tā jīntiān wǎnshang

就要到北京了，我想她現在一定很高興。"
jiù yào dào Běijīng le, wǒ xiǎng tā xiànzài yídìng hěn gāoxing."

布朗先生說：" 女兒很高興的時候，媽媽心裏很難過。"
Bùlǎng Xiānsheng shuō: "Nǚ'ér hěn gāoxing de shíhou, māma xīnli hěn nánguò."

布朗太太問丁雲：" 去年你來我們國家的時候，你媽媽願
Bùlǎng Tàitai wèn Dīng Yún: "Qùnián nǐ lái wǒmen guójiā de shíou, nǐ māma yuàn-

意你離開她嗎？"

yì nǐ líkāi tā ma?"

丁雲告訴布朗太太，她媽媽開始很高興，給她買了很多東
Dīng Yún gàosu Bùlǎng Tàitai, tā māma kāishǐ hěn gāoxìng, gěi tā mǎi le hěn duō dōng-

西。媽媽要她注意身體，努力學習，不要想家。她走的那天，
xi.   Māma yào tā zhùyì shēntǐ, nǔlì xuéxí, bú yào xiǎng jiā. Tā zǒu de nà tiān,

快上飛機了，她說"再見"，媽媽就哭了。
kuài shàng fēijī le, tā shuō "zàijiàn", māma jiù kū le.

"是啊！"布朗太太說。她又問："這兒離北京很遠，你
"Shì a!" Bùlǎng Tàitai shuō. Tā yòu wèn: "Zhèr lí Běijīng hěn yuǎn, nǐ

媽媽放心嗎？"
māma fàng xīn ma?"

丁雲說："我常常給媽媽寫信，告訴她這兒的老師和同學
Dīng Yún shuō: "Wǒ chángcháng gěi māma xiě xìn, gàosu tā zhèr de lǎoshī hé tóngxué

都很熱情，我在這兒過得很好。我還告訴媽媽，帕蘭卡是我的
dōu hěn rèqíng, wǒ zài zhèr guò de hěn hǎo.   Wǒ hái gàosu māma, Pàlánkǎ shì wǒ de

好朋友，她就像我的妹妹，她的家就像我自己的家。所以媽媽
hǎo péngyou, tā jiù xiàng wǒ de mèimei, tā de jiā jiù xiàng wǒ zìjǐ de jiā. Suǒyǐ māma

現在很放心。昨天我又寫信告訴他們，帕蘭卡快要去中國學習
xiànzài hěn fàng xīn. Zuótiān wǒ yòu xiě xìn gàosu tāmen, Pàlánkǎ kuài yào qù Zhōngguó xuéxí

了，她到了北京就要去看看媽媽。”

le, tā dào le Běijīng jiù yào qù kànkan māma."

布朗先生說：“ 帕蘭卡認識了一個中國姐姐，她到北京以

Bùlǎng Xiānsheng shuō: "Pàlánkǎ rènshi le yíge Zhōngguó jiějie, tā dào Běijīng yǐ-

後，又要認識一位中國媽媽。”

hòu, yòu yào rènshi yíwèi Zhōngguó māma."

布朗太太笑了。

Bùlǎng Tàitai xiào le.

二、生　詞

1.笑	xiào	to laugh, to smile
2.心	xīn	heart
3.送（人）	sòng (rén)	to see (walk) someone home, to see (someone) off
4.女兒	nǚ'er	daughter
5.去年	qùnián	last year
6.國家	guójiā	country
7.東西	dōngxi	thing
8.哭	kū	to cry, to weep
9.離	lí	from
10.遠	yuǎn	far, distant

11. 熱情	rèqíng	cordial, kind
12. 過	guò	to live, to get along
13. 自己	zìjǐ	self

三、注釋 Notes

1. "媽媽要她注意身體。"

"媽媽要她注意身體。" is a pivotal sentence in which the verb "要" is used in the sense of "to request" or "to ask".

2. "這兒離北京很遠。"

Prepositional constructions formed of the preposition "離" and its object often indicate distance in space or time, and the object may be either a noun of place or of time.

3. "她的家就像我自己的家。"

The pronoun "自己" is more often than not used in apposition to the pronoun or noun immediately preceding it for the sake of emphasis, e.g. "他自己", "大夫自己".

四、看圖會話 Talk About These Pictures

1. Request and prohibition

可以……嗎?

這兒不能……

2. Intention and possibility

她會來嗎?

她不會來,

她不想……

今晚電影

《大鬧天宮》

3. Ability

能當教練嗎？

4. Invitation and acceptance

能……嗎？

5. Entertaining a guest

請嘗嘗
請再吃一點兒……

6. Compliments and responses

漢字寫得……
哪裡，……

7. Talking about something done in the past

買了……

8. Talking about something that will take place in the future

車要……了

9. Talking about ball games

誰跟誰比賽?
誰贏了?
幾比幾?

10. Seeing someone off

要開車了,
要注意……
到了……請來信
祝你一路平安。

五、語法小結　A Brief Summary of Grammar

1.　The four kinds of simple sentences

According to the different component parts that make up their predicates, simple sentences fall into four different kinds:

(1)　Sentences with a nominal predicate

A sentence with a nominal predicate is one in which a noun, a nominal construction or a numeral-measure word serves as the main element of its predicate.　Sentences of this kind are usually used to state the time, someone's age or native place, etc.

現在三點。

今天星期五嗎？

我今年二十歲。

(2)　Sentences with a verbal predicate

Sentences in which verbs serve as the main element of the predicate occupy a dominant place in the Chinese language but are of a most complex character.　Ten different kinds of this type of sentences have been introduced so far (for detail see the following section).　More will be introduced in Book 2 of this reader.

我學習漢語。

她媽媽是大夫。

帕蘭卡有一個中國姐姐。

(3)　Sentences with an adjectival predicate

As far as their formation is concerned, sentences with an adjective as the main element of the predicate are very similar to sentences with an intransitive verb as the main element of the predicate (predicative adjectives may also take adverbial modifiers or complements).　"是" is not used in sentences of this type.

(534, 535, 536)

他很努力。

這兒離商店不遠。

(4) Sentences with a subject-predicate construction as their predicate

In sentences with subject-predicate constructions as their predicates we have come across, things indicated by the subjects of the subject-predicate constructions are parts of the things indicated by the subjects of the whole sentences, and the subject-predicate constructions are descriptive of the subjects of the whole sentences.

飛機上人真多。

布朗太太心裏很難過。

他工作怎麼樣?

2. Sentences with a verbal predicate (1)

1) "是" sentences

她是中國留學生。

這件襯衫不是新的。

2) "有" sentences

商店旁邊有一個餐廳。

他沒有哥哥。

3) Sentences without objects

他來了。

比賽要開始了。

4) Sentences with one object

我看了兩本畫報。

古波不認識他。

5) Sentences with two objects

王老師教他們語法。

丁雲送帕蘭卡一束花兒。

他告訴你他的名字了嗎?

6) Sentences with a verb or verbal construction as the object

現在開始上課。

他喜歡打乒乓球。

他會說漢語。

7) Sentences with a subject-predicate construction as the object

你知道他是誰嗎?

我想他現在一定很高興。

你媽媽願意你離開她嗎?

8) Sentences with a preposed object

他漢字寫得很好。

那本書你買了嗎?

9) Sentences with verbal constructions in series

媽媽進城買東西了。

我每天下午坐車去圖書館。

她送丁雲回學生宿舍。

10) Pivotal sentences

他們讓我唱一個歌兒。

我請我朋友吃飯。

布朗太太請丁雲坐她的車。

她媽媽要她注意身體。

3. Aspect particle " 了 " and modal particle " 了 " (1)

1) " 了 ", whether as an aspect particle or as a modal particle, is usually used in sentences with a verbal predicate. As an aspect particle, " 了 " comes after the verb, emphasizing that the action expressed by the verb has already been completed; as a modal particle, " 了 " is used to modify the entire statement, always found at the end of a sentence, emphasizing that the event referred to is something that has already taken place. E.g.

① 我看了今天的報沒有?

　　我看了（今天的報）。

② 下課以後你作什麼了?

　　我看報了。

Example ① stresses that the action expressed by the verb " 看 " has already been completed; Example ② stresses that the event expressed by " 看報 " has already taken place. If the aspect particle " 了 " is used to indicate the completion of an action, it usually implies that the entire event may not necessarily take place, as in "我下了課就進城". If it is stressed that the entire event has already occured, it is necessary to add the modal particle " 了 " at the end of the sentence, as in "我下了課就進城了".

In a sentence with the modal particle " 了 " to indicate that some event expressed by the whole sentence has already taken place, if the completion of the action expressed by the verb is specially emphasized, the aspect particle " 了 " is necessarily added after the verb. Compare:

① 你吃飯了嗎?
　　我吃飯了。
　　(A simple statement that some event has already taken place)

② 請在這兒吃飯吧?

－ 373 －　　　　　　　　　　(539, 540, 541)

謝謝，我吃了飯了。　　(A special emphasis that an action has already been completed)

(or)

我吃了。

What should be observed is that "了" is generally not used in simple statement of some past happening, i.e., when there is no need to stress its completion or occurance. E.g.

昨天上午他去中國大使館辦簽證，下午看足球賽。

2) When a verb takes after it both the aspect particle "了" and an object, the sentence remains an incomplete one except to possess one of the following requirements:

① The object is preceded by a numeral-measure word or other attributive. E.g.

我喝了一杯葡萄酒。

他買了很多中文雜誌。

她參觀了我們的宿舍。

② The object must be followed by another verb or a clause if it is a simple one. E.g.

明天我吃了飯就去看足球賽。

我參觀了工廠就回家了。

③ The object may be a simple one when the sentence ends with the modal particle "了". E.g.

他吃了飯了。

我看了電影了。

④ The object may be a simple one when the verb is preceded by a complicated adverbial adjunct. E.g.

布朗先生在機場給他們照了照片。

昨天他跟我們一起看了電影。

Points to be noted:

(1) Verbs not denoting actions such as "是", "在", "像" and "讓", and the verb "有" indicating existence, are never followed by the aspect particle "了".

(2) When a sentence with verbal constructions in series indicates the completion of an action, the aspect particle "了" is usually added after the second verb, e.g. "他去商店買了一雙冰鞋". It is incorrect to say "他去了商店買一雙冰鞋".

(3) When a monosyllabic verb is reduplicated, the aspect particle "了" should be inserted in between the two verbs, e.g. "他嘗了嘗茅台酒".

4. Optative verbs

(1) To indicate will or volition. E.g.

我要到機場送我朋友。 (The negative form of "要" is "不想".)

你想了解中國嗎?

他願意幫助我。

(2) To indicate ability or skill of a certain kind. E.g.

你能翻譯這本書嗎?

你可以翻譯這本書嗎? (The negative form of "可以" is "不能".)

他會滑冰。

(542, 543, 544)

(3) To indicate ability depending on circumstances. E.g.

明天你能來嗎?

明天你可以來嗎?

(The negative form of "可以" is "不能".)

能吸煙嗎?

可以吸煙嗎?

(4) To indicate probability or possibility. E.g.

他會去嗎?

(5) To indicate objective necessity. E.g.

學生要努力學習。

(The negative form of "要" is "不用".)

我們應該每天鍛鍊身體。

六、練習　Exercises

1. Give the antonym for each of the following adjectives and verbs:

新	笑
多	送
大	問
快	教
早	贏
難	來
高興	分別

2. Make sentences, using the groups of words and phrases given:

    (1) 請　　幫助

    (2) 坐車　去

    (3) 告訴　地址

    (4) 喜歡　看

    (5) 聽　　念課文

    (6) 要　　放心

    (7) 教　　開車

    (8) 給　　花兒

    (9) 問　　生詞

  (10) 注意　語法

3. Rewrite according to the instructions given in parentheses the following sentences using the aspect particle "了" to indicate that the action has been completed:

Example

        明天我看電影。

       (Supplying an attributive before the noun)

        你看不看?

     →昨天我看了那個電影。

        你看沒看?

    (1) 明天我參加比賽。

       (Adding the modal particle "了" to the verb)

        你參加不參加?

　　　　　　　　　　(545, 546)

(2) 晚上我作練習。

　　(Supplying another verb before the verb)

　　你作不作?

(3) 我辦簽證。

　　(Adding the modal particle "了" to the verb)

　　你辦不辦?

(4) 明天我看電視。　　(Supplying an adverbial of place)

　　你看不看?

(5) 晚上我作菜。

　　(Supplying an attributive before the noun)

　　你作不作?

(6) 星期天我聽唱片。　　(Supplying an adverbial adjunct)

　　你聽不聽?

4. Rearrange each of the following groups of words and phrases in a right order so as to make a sentence:

　　(1) 準備　行李　快　得　他　很

　　(2) 念　應該　課文　我們　常常

　　(3) 過　你們　好　星期天　嗎　得

　　(4) 還　這個　用　會　生詞　不　我

　　(5) 健康　身體　老師　我們　太　不

　　(6) 沒有　書　了　看　你　圖書館　到　昨天

　　(7) 多　房間　家　很　他

5. Put in prepositions in each of the following sentences:

　　(1) 我想＿＿＿＿你們照相。

(2) 他 _____ 帕蘭卡一起跳舞。

(3) 他們 _____ 這兒坐飛機到北京。

(4) 我朋友請我 _____ 他買一頂帽子。

(5) 學院 _____ 他家不太遠。

(6) 我常常 _____ 我朋友打電話。

(7) 他說 _____ 大家的健康乾杯。

(8) 我沒有 _____ 他寫信。

6. Translate the following into Chinese:

    (1) Can your friend go to the dance tomorrow?

    (2) Don't wait any longer. He is not likely to come today.

    (3) The doctor said that you should take good care of yourself.

    (4) How is he getting along with his studies of the problem?

    (5) He told me that he would leave shortly.

    (6) Are you willing to help me with my study of French?

7. Mark the following sentences, using (+) for the correct ones and (−) for the incorrect ones:

    (1) 這是誰的帽子呢? (　　)

    (2) 你想研究不研究中國文化? (　　)

    (3) 我去商店要買東西。(　　)

    (4) 你能用中文寫信嗎? (　　)

    (5) 我們上了飛機,就飛機起飛了。(　　)

    (6) 這個姑娘法語很好。(　　)

    (7) 我懂漢語語法一點兒。(　　)

    (8) 你們贏了還是輸了嗎? (　　)

    (9) 昨天我滑冰了,今天我要又滑冰。(　　)

(10) 他們星期三就要分別了。（　　）

8. Correct the following erroneous sentences.

　　(1) 晚上她寫了信。

　　(2) 明天我下了課就去看電影了。

　　(3) 昨天我去了他家的時候，他正看電視了。

　　(4) 去年我常常參加足球比賽了。

　　(5) 冬天我沒有滑冰了。

　　(6) 他起床了很早。

　　(7) 我想了看中國電影。

　　(8) 他們讓了我唱一個中國民歌。

　　(9) 代表團坐了飛機去中國。

　　(10) 有時候我跟他一起釣魚了。

　　(11) 老師問我了一個問題。

　　(12) 同學們都試試了中國筷子。

9. Write a short passage based on the pictures.